Sue Spence is a public speaker, v
educator who teaches communication ~~skills to corporate~~
groups and underprivileged youths using the principles of
Natural Horsemanship. Her business, Horses Helping Humans™,
and registered charity, the Horse Whispering Youth Program,
are built upon techniques she developed to help identify
individual personality profiles in conjunction with a person's
body language.

Sue works as a communications consultant with companies,
psychologists, psychiatrists, small businesses, schools and
community groups to help people unlock effective communication skills. She has over 40 years' equestrian experience
including show jumping and eventing, and has practiced
Natural Horsemanship for the past 20 years.

Sue is a recipricant of 2 Gold Coast Women In Business
Awards: Creating Change Award 2017 and Community
Dedication 2014 as well as 2018 Heart Of Women's Award
for Youth and Children's services. She holds a Diploma in
Child Youth and Family Intervention.

Horses Helping Humans™ is now a licensed program with
centers across Australia, New Zealand and now available for
world wide online certified training. Look for the Sue Spence
communications brand to ensure her original program is
being delivered. Visit the website www.horseshelpinghumans
australia.com for more info.

HORSES
WHO
HEAL

SUE SPENCE

First published 2016 in Macmillan by Pan Macmillan Australia Pty Ltd
1 Market Street, Sydney, New South Wales, Australia, 2000
Copyright © Sue Spence 2016

2nd Edition published by Suzanne Spence 2020
http://www.horseshelpinghumansaustralia.com/

The moral right of the author has been asserted.
Quote on pp 224-225 from 'An Interview with God', author unknown.

Prepublication Data Service is available
from the National Library of Australia
http://catalogue.nla.gov.au

ISBN: 978-0-6489660-0-5 (pbk)
ISBN: 978-0-6489660-1-2 (ebk)

Typeset in 13/19 pt Adobe Garamond by Midland Typesetters, Australia
Photo credits: Sue Spence unless otherwise indicated.

2020 updates by Publicious Book Publishing
http://www.publicious.com.au

The author and the publisher have made every effort to contact copyright
holders for material used in this book. Any person or organisation that
may have been overlooked should contact the publisher.

This book is dedicated to my beautiful mum and in memory of my dad – an absolute gentleman in every way. Their influence, acceptance, appreciation, encouragement, sense of humour, gratitude and compassion for others can be seen in my whole family, including my wonderful nieces and nephew and great nieces and nephew.

And to my beloved boys, Daniel and Jake.

PROLOGUE

I'm in New Zealand, where I was born and grew up, and it feels as though my life has come full circle.

I am visiting my cousin Joanne. She lives in Oxford in the South Island, coincidentally only twenty minutes from the pony camp I used to love as a child. Joanne's property is beautiful, with the Southern Alps as a backdrop and lush horse paddocks surrounded by pine trees.

We are reminiscing about our childhood as we wander down to say hello to her cherished horses. They all come running to the fence to greet us. All except one: a dapple grey standing on his own under a tree. He is not interacting with the rest of the herd and has no interest in approaching us. Immediately I am

1

curious, because his behaviour and body language are indicating that something isn't quite right.

Joanne tells me that his name is Fred and she thinks he's depressed because he stands under the same tree all day. He won't interact with her and he has no interest in being caught. Joanne is one of the most gentle, loving people towards horses, so it is very strange that he doesn't want to connect with her.

When I ask about his background, she tells me that she bought him from someone on the west coast who practised Natural Horsemanship. As soon as I hear that, my ears prick up. When horses have been trained the Natural Horsemanship way, they respond to different signals. If Fred has been trained this way, he needs someone who speaks his language. And it just so happens that I do.

As I approach Fred, he puts his ears back and walks away from me. So I breathe out, turn around and walk away from him. We repeat this a couple of times until something clicks and he realises we share the same language. Before too long he is following me. After he has followed me for a few steps, I stand quietly until he touches me with his nose. We stand like this for a little while, with me making no effort to touch him.

Then, I hold the rope halter open in front of me and he slowly puts his nose into it. Then, just as slowly, I very gently pass the rope up over his head and do up the halter. I can hear Joanne saying from the gate, 'Oh, that's amazing.'

I am thrilled but of course I can't show it as I don't want to frighten him. To feel him starting to connect with me, and to know that he realises I can speak his language, is beautiful.

Before too long, Fred is trotting around me when I ask him to circle me; he's walking sideways for me, backing up beautifully and then gently coming back in when I ask him. We play in this manner for nearly an hour and to see his eyes brighten and his ears prick forward, to see the change in this majestic horse, is heart-warming.

Here I am back in Oxford, a place that holds so many good horse memories, and I'm doing what I love the most – connecting with a horse. It has been a long journey back to this place, a journey that has seen me struggle with illness and anxiety and depression, but at last I have recovered my sense of wellbeing and happiness. I really have come full circle.

CHAPTER 1

'Can I please have a white pony?' These are the first words I can remember saying. Birthdays and Christmases passed with wonderful presents – bikes, dolls, dollhouses – but each time I would think, *Love my presents, but where's the white pony?*

It was such a strong yearning, it was almost overwhelming. Even at that young age I knew life would not be complete for me until I had a horse. I constantly imagined a little white pony who was my very best friend. I didn't understand why at that age, of course, but now it is plain to me that horses and ponies were always going to play a big part in my emotional health and healing.

It was forty years before I got my white pony but there were many other ponies and horses throughout that time that touched my heart and, without my realising it, formed the foundation of the work I do today.

I believe that people are born with the horse gene. There is neither rhyme nor reason why a love for horses and riding completely possesses you from a young age and in no way fades as you grow up. Once it possesses you, it possesses you forever. I have heard all sorts of stories from other 'horse-mad' people about the levels they have gone to just to be near a horse, and how even the smell of a horse will make them swoon with happiness. I know exactly how they feel.

I grew up in Christchurch, New Zealand, and it was the perfect place to follow my horsey passion. There were spectacular forests filled with the fresh tang of pine trees to ride through; deserted beaches with high tussocky sandhills to gallop along, tracks meandering through rolling green vistas to amble across.

I had my first riding lesson when I was four years old. It had taken a great deal of persuasion – or a great deal for a small child, anyway – to get my parents to agree. I remember being so excited I could hardly breathe. Sitting still in the back of Dad's Vauxhall was nearly impossible. When we arrived at the riding school nestled in the beautiful Christchurch foothills, I was disappointed to discover that my first lesson was to be on a forty-four gallon drum turned on its side, with what looked like a giant rolling pin underneath it and a little saddle on top.

I was thinking at the time, *But I want to get on a real horse!* However, once it was explained to me that learning on the barrel would help make me a good rider by getting me used to the way a horse moves, I settled down. It was actually an excellent idea as it helped develop my balance. The instructor gently moved the roller under the drum, which replicated the movement of a horse. Just to be sitting on a real saddle, knowing it was the start of learning to ride, plus having a big cuddle with one of the ponies, was enough for me on that first day.

It wasn't long, however, before my instructor could see that my balance was good enough for me to progress to a real live pony. Within a couple of weeks I was sitting on Blackie, a beautiful little black pony who gently taught me to ride. Even in those early days I wanted to spend time talking to Blackie before I got on his back. I wanted to know what his favourite foods were and who his friends were. When I come to think of it, I was the only child interested in every detail of Blackie's life; the others just wanted to get on and ride. Even back then it was about the relationship, not just the riding.

I realise now that when I was growing up all of my favourite books and TV shows were about connecting to and understanding animals on a deeper level. They were about the relationship between animals and people, about trust and love and respect. I seemed to realise intuitively that animals had feelings and had emotional reactions to their surroundings. *My Friend Flicka*, *Lassie*, *Black Beauty* and, of course, my favourite TV show

Mr Ed (it seemed perfectly normal to me to have a horse living in your house, talking to you!) – all of them explored a deep connection between humans and their animals.

Natural Horsemanship was not well known in New Zealand in those days. We were all trained in the same style at pony clubs and riding schools in those early years, with the emphasis on your riding position rather than how your horse was feeling. Even so, all the foundations of Natural Horsemanship – trust, connection and respect – were right there in my understanding of how it should be between horses and humans.

In *Black Beauty* I used to cry every time Beauty was sold because he was taken away from his friends. No matter how many times I read the book, I still cried! But now I understand that the bond horses forge with one another is so strong, particularly when they have a paddock mate, that when they are separated it causes them a great deal of anxiety and sadness. In an established herd, each horse knows where it belongs and is accepted, and this creates security and safety. It should be the same in human families: acceptance, respect and trust. I was so lucky because these values were instilled in me by the family I was brought up in.

My family is English and they moved to New Zealand in 1959. I was born in 1961, the only Kiwi of the bunch. My sister is eleven years older than me, and my brother nine years older. Even though I was so much younger, I never felt that I was in the way as some younger siblings feel with their older brothers and sisters – except when I wanted to join in on my brother's Monopoly games with his friends. In England, Dad was a Rolls Royce mechanic and had his own specialised business. In fact he looked after the British royal family's fleet of Rolls Royces. He often told funny stories of servicing the cars and then taking them for a test run through country lanes. Once he was pulled over by the police when he was driving Princess Margaret's car, as he had accidentally left the royal flag flying. There was my dad, driving the royal Rolls around the neighbourhood, looking like he had stolen it!

My mum and dad met during the Second World War. Dad was a mechanic and was posted to India with the Royal Air Force. He had the job of repairing the aircraft and ensuring they were running safely. When he was returning to London at the end of the war, he met Mum at a railway station. My mum told me that this particular day the train was running very late and she noticed a handsome man with beautiful dark wavy hair who kept looking at her. She was also sneaking glances at him and, as the train was so late, they eventually started chatting, and there a love story began.

At the time, my mum was doing accounting work for a very successful businessman; she was also in the Land Army and actively involved in helping with food distribution. Hearing Mum and Dad's stories of the Second World War has always given me a great appreciation of how easy our lives are now. The stories of blackouts, bombings, hiding in bomb shelters and food restrictions were very real to me as it was my own mum and dad who lived through those dreadful war years.

After Mum and Dad were married they lived in Chiswick in a beautiful Tudor-style house. My sister, Pam, remembers little garden parties, a massive tortoise as her pet and spending time in the Royal Park Garden and in Hyde Park. She was one of the youngest children ever to be accepted into the Royal Ballet School in London. When my brother, Peter, was young, he had a heart murmur and the doctors recommended that Mum and Dad move to a warmer climate to help improve his health. So when my brother was about seven years old, they picked New Zealand. Of course, there was a lack of Rolls Royces in Christchurch so Dad became a heating engineer, but he never stopped tinkering with cars. I remember the times I would hear Mum calling out, 'Where's my good cutlery?' only to find Dad had it out in his tool box, because in those days, when you tinkered, you tinkered properly. Everything was done by hand.

My dad's sister, Aunty Peg, and her husband George followed my parents to New Zealand, travelling overland in a Bedford Van. They travelled for six months through Europe, Iran, India and many other countries, and Aunty Peg documented their adventures in a book she wrote in 1999 entitled *Our Journey – Half Circle*. My father's brother, Uncle Bob, his wife Hazel and their children followed a few years later, prompted by the difficult economic situation in England.

Being a classic English family, weekends were all about picnics and outings. In the summer we would go for a picnic by the beach every Sunday, and I have a lasting image of my mum and dad sitting in deckchairs at the edge of the sea, their feet in the water, Dad with his trousers rolled up to his knees and the pair of them wearing hats made out of newspaper or big handkerchiefs with knots tied in the corners. They might have been in New Zealand, but you could still pick the English people! Picnics were always about beautiful food and Mum prepared a huge array of food: quiche, bacon and egg pie, sandwiches, salad fresh from the garden, roast chicken, apple pie, her famous fruitcake and home-baked biscuits, jam tarts and her amazing home-grown rhubarb pie, all of which would be spread out across brightly checked rugs and would disappear at an alarming rate.

One day we were on our way to the beach and Mum and Dad noticed an open gate that led to a lush field. They had unloaded us children and all the picnic gear, spread out the picnic blankets on the top of a gentle rise and put out all of the food, cutlery and plates, when a tractor came chugging towards us. 'This is actually private property and I need to plough this field,' said the farmer, so we had to pack it all up and move on. We were laughing all the way home, remembering the look on the farmer's face when he saw a whole family settled in, surrounded by beautiful food and silver cutlery, picnicking on his land.

Even though we lived in town, it seemed as though we were living in the country. We always had lots of animals and dogs, and when I was very young we had chickens in the backyard and a huge vegetable patch. My mum and dad were brilliant gardeners and our garden was so beautiful. Their vegetable patches looked like market gardens. The rest of the garden looked like the Royal Botanical Gardens. My mum and sister used to take me to the shops with me sitting up in my huge old-fashioned pram, in a bright frilly hat, accompanied by two chickens (which my sister dressed up in hats and capes) and the cat. The animals never jumped out but caused a lot of attention. Our chickens all had names and one, Penny, used to lay her egg every morning on Dad's garage workbench. Animals with personalities and emotions were perfectly normal to me, and I'm grateful for the way I was brought up respecting and appreciating animals, as it laid the foundation for what I do today.

My father was a respectful, gentle man. Mum has constantly been warm and giving, and my brother, with his fantastic sense of humour, and my kind, loving older sister have continually made me feel secure. My sister, who is a talented artist, painted my bedroom with amazing fairytale murals. When I was three the whole family helped my dad build me a little wooden horse with wheels. My sister even made the saddle and bridle. It put the biggest smile on my face. To me, that was my first horse!

However, my yearning for a real horse was always present. It was all I'd think about, and even though I was so young,

I knew I was going to have horses in my life one day. I would be watching the old Westerns that were on TV, shows like *The High Chaparral* and *Bonanza*, with my eyes glued to the horses. I thought Zorro's bond with his horse was amazing and I used to imagine having the same bond with my own horse. Even though we had dogs, cats, birds, an eel that I fed daily (his name was Sammy) and guinea pigs that I used to bring inside to sit and watch *Bonanza* and *The High Chaparral* with me, it never stopped the yearning for my own pony.

As a family, we would watch *The Wonderful World of Disney*, play Monopoly and checkers and have dress-up parties for birthdays. Mum and Dad would organise egg and spoon races, sack races, sing songs and we would all put on a performance and receive a prize. There was lots of laughter and Mum and Dad looked on the bright side of everything. I have such a big place in my heart for the young people who come to me now who haven't been so fortunate to grow up in a loving family. They miss out on the self-worth and self-confidence developed through the kind of encouragement and support that was natural to my parents. It is a privilege to be able to teach these young people about respect and trust and how to accept each other in all their differences, and to show them that when they have children of their own, they can raise them on these foundations.

As easily as I connect with animals, I seem to be able to connect to the students who come to us with enormous personal challenges. The success of our Horses Helping Humans™ program has in part been because of my ability to almost feel what they are feeling. I was first conscious of my acute sensitivity when I was very young, but I didn't understand what it was back then. I often experienced this sensitivity with animals; somehow I just knew when they were happy or sad.

I used to stay the night at a friend's house, and there was a little pony in a nearby paddock. I visited this pony every time I went to play with my friend. I would think about him constantly as I instinctively knew that he was lonely. I could feel his sorrow coming with me whenever I said goodbye to him. I would tell my friend how sad he was and she would say to me, 'Don't be silly, he's just a pony. There's nothing wrong with him, he's happy just eating grass.' But I knew he wasn't.

One day I was giving him a cuddle from my side of the fence when the woman who owned him turned up. It was the first time I had seen her. I stood back and watched as she went into his paddock to fill up his water trough, and I could clearly see on his little face that he was very uncomfortable around her; to me he looked scared. I had not seen that expression on his face before; up until then I had only noticed how sad he looked when I left, or how happy he looked when I arrived. I was convinced that the pony needed rescuing! I informed my friend that we were going to rescue the pony and find him a happy home. I had no idea how we would do this, all I knew was that I had to make the pony happy.

I asked my friend's brother if I could borrow one of his belts and could he also possibly find me a torch. I had acquired both by bedtime and I told my friend that we were going to wait until everyone was asleep before we went to rescue the pony. Well, her dad heard us fluffing around in the bedroom as we tried to get changed out of pyjamas in the dark, and all my plans for saving the pony came to an abrupt end!

CHAPTER 2

Life seemed to be filled with many wonderful colours and activities, and I was able to be outside as often as I wanted, playing and interacting with all the animals we had at home. That all changed on my first day at school. I remember Mum was standing at the door to the classroom I was meant to enter. I was hiding behind her, clutching her skirt. I didn't want to go into that room. Even back then I remember thinking that the windows were too small. I liked lots of light and fresh air, and there were too many people in the room. I felt overwhelmed.

Sitting still for long periods of time was a challenge for me. Right from the start of my schooling life I was constantly in trouble for fidgeting. I didn't understand how the other children could sit still for so long. I didn't understand how you could put up with being inside all day, without being able to run outside whenever you wanted, to feel the sun on your face, the grass under your bare feet, to be able to watch the clouds drifting across the sky and enjoy listening to the birds singing. For as long as I can remember, to be in nature has been as important to me as breathing.

My style of learning was different from most other children's, but no one understood that then. I was judged as not being able to absorb anything I was being taught, yet when I was sitting in the back of the car when Mum and Dad went for drives, I always remembered the directions everywhere we went, even if we had only been there once. Mum and Dad would be puzzling over maps and I would pipe up from the back seat like a little human GPS, 'You need to turn left at the big oak tree, and then you need to turn right at the big paddock with the shed.' Clearly there was not a problem with my memory but with the way I absorbed things when they were taught in a particular way.

I recently found some storybooks that I had written at school when I was about seven years old. In the front of one was a list of topics I wanted to write about. My first topic was (of course!) horses; second was animals, then the wind, followed by the clouds. So when the teachers would say, 'Suzanne' – they always used my full name when I was in trouble – 'focus and listen, you are away with the fairies,' they were absolutely right. I would have been daydreaming about riding horses with the wind in my hair and the clouds racing through the sky.

Something else that stood out when I found these books was the list I had to write of 'things that make me sad'. Looking at that list now, it amazes me why a little girl would even be thinking about such things. They included 'when I see a dead animal on the road, I feel so so sad because someone has run it over and it has been left there . . . The noise of a fire engine, makes me so, so sad, because someone's house is on fire and all of their things will be burnt . . . When I hear of wars, I don't feel very happy, because I hear of people getting killed, it is so sad when I hear of people getting diseases.' Perhaps these days, when a child is exposed to a barrage of media coverage of dreadful events around the world, it might be understandable to be worried about such things, but back then we never watched the news or saw distressing events on television, and we never talked about upsetting things at home. It must have been my own acute sensitivity.

The item at the bottom of the list of things that made me sad took me right back to when I first started getting bullied at school: 'When someone is calling me names and hitting me, I feel sad because if I tell anyone, they will get even nastier.'

I remember Mum telling a boy off after school one day because he had been calling me names and pushing me. I didn't want to say anything, but on this particular day I was even more upset than usual, so I told my mum. She used to walk me to and from school every day and on the way home we would always stop at a little cake shop. That day the boy walked into the shop when we were in there, and Mum could tell by the look on my face that he was the bully. She gave him a good telling-off – in a very dignified English manner!

As I grew older, the bullying became more persistent. Perhaps it was because, due to my English upbringing, I spoke a little differently and used different words. In one of my storybooks I described something as 'absolutely ghastly', which would not have been the words that most young New Zealand children would have been using at the time. Also, I was short-sighted and had to wear glasses in class. In those days they were the horn-rimmed, Coke-bottle-bottom type and I was made fun of every time I put them on to see the blackboard.

I remember very clearly feeling bullied by certain teachers. I really did try my best to sit still and listen, but there were some teachers who had no understanding of how hard that was for me. They would yell at me, make me sit in the corner in front of the whole class, and some would smack me across the palm with a ruler, all because I didn't know how to sit still for a long time and stay focused. I wouldn't have known how to articulate the feelings this invoked in me back then, but they were a mixture of humiliation, confusion and anxiousness. I always felt like it wasn't fair. Schools didn't have counsellors in those days but I would have benefited greatly by having someone to talk to and to explain that I simply have to learn things in a different way to most other people.

My inability to sit still and focus was not really noticed before I started school because the whole house was so full of activity. I was either helping Mum in the garden or with the animals, or tinkering with Dad in his garage. My brother had a little rowboat that he absolutely loved, and he would often be looking for an excuse to take Mum and I to the shop in it so he could row us up the river. My sister loved painting things or making beautiful clothes, and I would happily bounce from one activity to the next. Having to sit and concentrate on one topic for a whole hour was like torture to me!

It makes sense to me now why I felt more comfortable with animals than I did with humans, because I felt a little different. I was anxious around people in a way I never was around animals. And when you are a little bit different, it tends to attract bullies. I was picked on from a very early age at school as I wasn't very good at standing up for myself. Any sort of confrontation made me incredibly uncomfortable, so I would do my best to avoid it. I was brought up in a house where we never really had any confrontation, so it was something I just didn't understand or know how to deal with.

Even when I went to school camp, I was bullied. One of the girls had seen me scream when a big moth flew into my cabin one night, so the next night she and her friend collected as many moths as they could and filled my sleeping bag with them. When I turned out the light and went to get into my sleeping bag, the terror was overwhelming. I didn't tell anyone, though, as I didn't want to get into more trouble with the bullies.

I was so desperate to fit in at school that I tried to make friends with all the full-on personalities. Deep down I was intimidated by them, but instead of keeping away from them and making friends with people I felt more comfortable with, I tried to appease them by becoming part of their group. They were all quite impressed by the amount of times I was sent out of the classroom, although I wasn't being sent out for being naughty or disrespectful but because I couldn't keep still. They felt that I belonged in their group, but I knew I was different to them. I didn't let it show, though, because I was so scared of being bullied again. I wished both groups could just join together and we could all be friends. I couldn't understand then why, at recess, one lot of students would sit on one side, feeling intimidated, while the other group were picking on them.

It was normal for me to chat about the relationship between my horse and me, but I suppose back then, communication with animals was not often spoken of. I would be teased with comments like 'Sue thinks her horse talks to her', or 'Sue thinks she can talk to a horse'. What I couldn't articulate then was that it was about the energy – I felt the connection between myself and my horse. There were times when we thought and moved as one. But most of the children just didn't get it.

A lot of the students I work with now who have been badly bullied tend to put themselves in a similar situation so that they can feel as though they fit in. It's like the old saying: 'If you can't beat them, join them.' But this is totally wrong. It's not about having to beat anyone. It's about having self-respect and self-confidence so that you can make good choices and stand up for yourself.

I had some quieter friends and it was lovely to be able to talk to them about connecting with animals and the beauty of horses. I would often bring other children, who had been bullied, home to meet our animals to try to cheer them up. When I had been bullied, I would go to my horses for comfort. I would sit out in the paddock, close to my horse, and feel all the stress and tension leaving my body. It was like stepping into a different world. When I was with my horses, I felt accepted, confident and happy.

My weekly riding lesson was what I looked forward to most every week. A week between riding lessons is an extremely long time to a horse-mad eight-year-old! After that first wonderful relationship with Blackie, I was ready to move up to a more advanced riding school. It was sad knowing I wouldn't be riding Blackie regularly any more, but I knew I could visit him whenever I liked. The new riding school was at a place called Hallswell. My new riding partner was Bracken, a beautiful gentle gelding with a white blaze down his face and two tiny white socks on his back legs. Recently I was thrilled to find an old photo of me sitting on Bracken and wearing the special green jumper my mum knitted for me to wear to riding lessons. I still have it stored safely away.

At this stage, I was learning to canter and pop over small jumps. I know my mum was always anxious about me jumping, and this anxiety increased for her as I got older and the jumps got bigger. Dad was always quietly confident in me. This was the start of my great love for showjumping and eventing, though it would be quite a few years before I would enter my first showjumping ring.

Around this time, I kept seeing advertisements for a school holiday pony camp. I remember showing Mum and begging to go, but she was hesitant at the thought of my staying away from home on my own, which I'd never done before. But after driving out to meet the lovely people who ran the camp, she was reassured that I would be in safe hands. I started going to pony camp from the age of nine through to fifteen and would stay from anywhere between seven to fourteen days. It never took long to make friends with the girls there, as everyone was as horse-mad as I was.

I would count down the days to school holidays when I could go to camp and I was always packed days before I was due to leave. Mum tells me that every time we sat down for dinner, all I would talk about was horses and how long it was until I went to camp. For me, getting out of the classroom environment and spending all day everyday outside with my horse was absolute heaven. At pony camp I never felt different, or incapable of learning. I was so confident and focused on the new techniques we were being taught, I began to understand that I was quite capable of learning in the right environment.

The pony camp where I spent most school holidays was nestled at the foot of the Southern Alps, in Oxford, one of the most picturesque pieces of country you will find in the South Island of New Zealand, and the place where my cousin Joanne settled years later. It was called Kowhai Pony Camp and it is still running now as the Kowhai Residential School of Riding. Mornings at pony camp were filled with our lessons. Straight after breakfast we would bring our horses in from the paddocks and spend time brushing them and then saddling up. We would start with a gentle warm-up in one of the arenas and then we would progress to the dressage ring, and by the end of the morning we would go into the jumping arena where lots of little coloured jumps were set up. After lunch we would trek through the countryside, riding through creeks, popping our horses over little logs and cantering across the countryside. The farmland we used to ride through every afternoon had the mountains in the background, and the only sound we could hear when we were riding was the clip-clopping of the horses' hooves, the bleating of sheep across the hills and the chirping of birds.

The pony I was first matched with was Judy. She was little, brown and quite tubby, and she was getting on in years, but she was very safe and very kind and I felt completely at ease on her.

The horsemanship I developed at pony camp was due to the expert tuition I received from Liz Thomas, who, with her husband Bruce, ran Kowhai. Liz is a performance coach in showjumping, dressage and eventing. Having two weeks at a time to practise all the techniques meant I improved at a much greater rate than when I was having just one lesson a week. For days at a time I was completely immersed in all aspects of riding and handling horses, with such a fabulous, skilled and generous instructor and no outside distractions – not that anything could have distracted me at that time! Their beautiful property was a horsey home away from home, and Liz and Bruce's warmth and encouragement has stayed with me to this day. I believe my eventual success in showjumping and eventing was the result of that wonderful opportunity.

After years of riding lessons and pony camp, I was more desperate than ever for a horse or pony of my own. I was constantly searching through the horses-for-sale column of the local newspaper. One day I cut out a notice for a buckskin horse named Sandy, advertised for eighty dollars, and showed it to Mum and Dad in the hope that, if it wasn't too expensive, they might agree to my dream coming true. They realised by now that my love of horses was not going to wear off; in fact, it was getting stronger and stronger as I grew older. After much pleading, my parents agreed to go and have a look at the horse. Most of the drive on the way to see him went along the lines of, 'Do you realise how much work is going to be involved if you have a horse? You are going to have to feed him twice a day, clean the paddock, look after his feet, put rugs on and take them off, and change his water daily.' I was bouncing about on the back seat of the car with, 'I promise I will do that every day.' I would have been happy to do all of those jobs four times a day if meant me having my very own horse!

As soon as I laid eyes on Sandy, I knew I had to have him. When Mum and Dad agreed, I couldn't believe it was true. I was finally going to have my own horse! We rented a paddock for him that was only a half-hour bike ride away from our house. I couldn't wait to get there in the mornings and the evenings, to do all the jobs Mum and Dad thought would be chores for me but which turned out to be work that I loved. Even having my own grooming kit, saddle and bridle was almost more excitement than this ten-year-old could bear. I remember wishing that Sandy lived in our back garden so I never had to leave him. My dream of having a property where my horse lived with me started way back then.

Once I had Sandy, Mum enrolled me into the local pony club. I would ride there every Sunday without fail. The excitement would start as soon as I got up and dressed in my pony club uniform of a white long-sleeved shirt and tie and maroon jumper and my jodhpurs and boots. Once I got to the paddock, I would spend ages brushing Sandy and making sure all of my gear was clean and ready to be inspected at the start of our pony club lessons.

Even though my weekends and daylight hours after school were consumed by Sandy, I had a problem that I didn't want anyone to know about. Sandy bucked, and he bucked pretty hard! I didn't want Mum to find out because I was terrified she would insist he be sold. The funny thing was, he only bucked when I was out riding by myself; he never tried it at pony club or camp.

In fact, I really advanced my jumping technique on Sandy at pony camp. I recently came across a photograph of us jumping at camp in 1971. I wish I had told my instructors about Sandy's bucking issue. They would have had some great advice on how to handle the situation. But I was too scared to tell anybody in case it got back to Mum and Dad that he may not be safe for me to ride. On one occasion, I was bucked off and knocked unconscious. A kindly farmer and his wife took me into their house and gave me some water. They asked me for my parents' phone number so they could call them and tell them about the accident, but I wouldn't give it to them. I just wanted to get back to the paddock before anyone found out what had happened.

A few months later, Mum was watching me riding Sandy quietly around the paddock when he decided it might be rather fun to go into a bucking frenzy. I flew over his head, much to my mother's horror, landing head first with so much force that the button on the top of my riding helmet cut my head open. After Mum saw that, there was no negotiation about whether I could continue to ride Sandy: he had to be sold. We found him a loving home with an experienced rider who was capable of re-educating him that it was not appropriate to buck off your rider. Even though he went to a good home I spent what felt like weeks crying myself to sleep. The gap Sandy left in my life was something that could only be filled by another horse. The horse that filled this gap and caused my heart to overflow with love was to come into my life sooner than I expected.

CHAPTER 3

When I had Sandy I was still in junior high school. I struggled with so many of the subjects because I couldn't seem to concentrate. The more I tried to take in what the teachers were saying, the less I heard. The more I tried to sit still and read what was on the blackboard, the less I saw. I was always anxious about going to school, as I knew each day would be another struggle to learn.

Although I found subjects like maths and science impossible, I loved reading. Library time was my favourite. I would take out as many horse books as I was allowed and immerse myself in their world. I seemed to wait all day for the going-home bell to ring so that I could race off to be with my horse, and then when I got home I would dive straight back into my horse books. The only time I seemed to be able to concentrate was when I was having something to do with my horses.

I didn't say too much to Mum and Dad about this as I thought it was just the way things were. However, they were aware of what was going on as they were so many teachers' notes coming home. The fact that I was so happy and enthusiastic around horses yet so stressed and anxious when I was at school was concerning them greatly. Mum informs me that they would go to meeting after meeting trying to work out what the problem was. Apparently Dad even attended Parent-Teacher Association meetings and often he would be the only man there.

I still felt like I didn't fit in with any of the groups, plus I seemed to get bullied a fair bit. I was the only person in my class to have a horse, and my classmates probably didn't understand why I was so obsessed with him. I made friends with other girls who shared the horse paddock we rented for Sandy. Unfortunately these girls went to a different school. We would often ride together and take our horses to the beach and to Pony Club. I had one really close friend who didn't have a horse but absolutely loved them and we would collect horse ornaments and knick-knacks. Her parents were not in the position to get her a horse of her own, so she really appreciated being able to spend time with mine. I loved sharing my horsey world with her as I understood the yearning she had to be around horses.

I think my parents understood how alienated I felt at school and how important my relationships with horses was, because even though they were both very nervous about my finding another horse, they agreed to let me start looking – the only stipulation was that I was to find a smaller horse.

We went out to a property in a little town called Kaipoi, which is about half an hour out of Christchurch, to have a look at a pony that had been advertised for sale in the local newspaper. I was beside myself with excitement, already dressed in my jodhpurs and riding boots. The property was absolutely gorgeous. It looked more like an English estate. It had stables with half-doors and lush rolling paddocks, one of which was filled with jumps. The man who owned the property was a highly respected showjumper and trainer. While he went off to catch the pony, I caught sight of a beautiful big bay horse, at least sixteen hands high, with a white blaze down her face. She was in a yard close to where Dad had parked the car. It was an overcast, cloudy day, typical of the South Island, but when I looked over to her it was like the sun had come out. Once she turned her face towards me, something happened. I could see in her, as she could see in me, that we had the same gentleness, and somehow we understood immediately that we would be safe with each other. I tried to focus on the demonstration the man was giving us with the pony, but my eyes kept going back to her, and her eyes never left me either. There was no question of my leaving there without her, so it was just as well she was for sale too.

My parents were, of course, very keen for me to ride the pony, but I begged them to let me ride the bay to see how we would get on together. From the moment I got on her back, we were the perfect fit. It was as though we had been riding together forever. As soon as we started moving around the paddock, we just flowed. I was more comfortable on her than I had been on any other horse before, and I could feel she was totally comfortable with me. It was as though we were soul mates. Her nature was so loving, but she had an amazing energy; she seemed to float when she moved. She radiated everything I had imagined a horse to be: strong yet light, majestic yet gentle. I had been so desperately looking for my own special horse, and it seemed to me that she had been waiting for her own special human.

Mum and Dad were hesitant about buying such a big horse for me, but after assurances from her owner that she was very trustworthy, they agreed to the purchase. I named her Lady because she had such a graceful dignity about her. The day we went to pick her up was so exciting. I couldn't believe I was going to have such a wonderful horse all of my own. My sister, even though she wasn't horsey, came with us as she knew how thrilled I was and wanted to share the experience. Pam has always been elegant and beautiful, and when I look at a photo of that day I realise how glamorous she looked, as befitted meeting Lady for the first time!

It was Lady who taught me about a real connection with horses. Our relationship was so close that I was convinced we were telepathically connected. I even wrote to an author in England who had written a book called *Talking with Horses* which was all about how he connected with horses, as I had to try to share my experience with someone who would understand. When I rode Lady through the pine forests alongside the beach, I would think to myself, *Lady, let's go left at the next turn.* I wouldn't even pick up my reins and she would turn left. Now that I understand Natural Horsemanship and the amazing sensitivity of horses, I realise that as I was thinking *Let's go left*, I would have made the slightest movement with my body and she responded to that.

Lady had such an amazing energy and movement when I rode her that it honestly felt like I was flying. We would gallop down the beach and through the sand tracks of the pine forest and her long legs would extend out smoothly and lightly as though we were skimming along the ground, perfectly at one with each other. The times we spent riding along the beach together, cantering at the water's edge, and enjoying gentle rides through the forest are my fondest memories of our special times together.

The relationship I had with Lady was so important during my first year of high school as I was once again subjected to bullying. It was so bad that Mum used to walk me to the bus stop in the morning and meet me off the bus when

I got home, even though I was thirteen years old. There was a gang of kids that used to verbally threaten me, promising that they would 'get me' after school. Mum went in to discuss the bullying with the headmaster, even though I had asked her not to as I was scared they would find out I had told on them. I was so scared of speaking up then, but I now realise that the first thing you must do if you are bullied, as an adult or a child, is tell someone you can trust. Because I didn't speak up soon enough, I constantly felt sick and fearful.

All I wanted to do was to be with Lady, where I knew I was safe. I lost so much confidence, as you do when you have been bullied, and the only time I felt strong and powerful was when I was with her. When I was riding Lady, she made me feel that, as a team, we were invincible and no one could hurt us or make me feel scared.

Lady's previous owner had been a successful showjumper and had trained many horses for the show ring. Clearly he didn't think Lady had the ability for a successful showjumping career, perhaps because she could be quite nervous and highly strung. It turned out, though, that she had an amazing natural ability and ease for jumping. Her jump was incredible. It felt like we were flying. I spent many hours with a wonderful instructor to perfect our jumping technique, and after a few months my confidence, and Lady's, grew enormously. As our partnership was so strong we became very successful on the local showjumping circuit, and on one occasion we placed first in a competition in which her previous owner was also competing. He approached me at that show and said with a smile, 'I wish I hadn't sold her.' I remember thinking to myself, *Lady jumps like she does because we have such a beautiful relationship.*

For the few years that I had Lady, we regularly came home from competitions with ribbons. By the time I was fourteen I had completed all of my relevant certificates at pony club, which included Levels of Riding, Horse Care and Instructing, and I was then able to start teaching riding.

I leased a couple of little ponies that were suitable for teaching youngsters so I could give lessons. My classes were popular because I was teaching my students not only to ride but also how to care for horses and be safe around them. I was in my element. I felt that helping people with horses was my purpose. I could be myself, and I didn't have to worry about not being capable of learning things I wasn't even interested in. The person I was around horses, doing what I loved, and the anxious confused person I was at school were polar opposites. So I think it's true to say that horses are the reason I have developed into the person that I am today.

Mum and Dad were always towing the horse float around to local shows, in all types of weather. My brother and sister were both married by this stage, so Mum and Dad were free to travel with me, and they enjoyed show days as much as I did. Some shows would become a real family outing, with even my aunt and uncle and their family coming to share one of Mum's big picnics in some of the most picturesque pony clubs around the South Island.

The South Island of New Zealand is the most amazing place to compete in cross-country events. Galloping through scenery with the snow-covered Alps in the background and flying over ditches, logs, gates and through creeks was challenging and invigorating all at the same time. I absolutely loved my jumping but I always struggled with dressage as I had to focus long enough to remember the dressage test selected for each competition. A dressage test is similar to learning a choreographed dance. Letters of the alphabet are marked around the perimeter of the arena and the test may ask you to enter the arena at A, halt at X, then proceed to C, and so on. My brain doesn't do well following complex instructions, and a dressage test has to be done exactly as it is written out, you cannot divert from it in any way. I always felt a lot of pressure entering the dressage arena as I knew I could not make a single mistake. At some shows, we were allowed to have a caller, so someone stood at one end of the arena and called out your next move for you. Boy, did I enjoy the difference that made!

Even walking the course before a showjumping event was a challenge for me as I had to remember the jump sequence.

I would always wonder how other competitors could remember the order of jumps when they only walked the course once, whereas I had to walk it two or three times. That was why one of my favourite events was called Hit and Hurry. When you entered the arena, you chose which jumps you wanted to tackle and in which order, as it was judged on time. Lady and I both loved the showjumping and cross-country components, so our points were always high in those areas, but we lost points in dressage. We still placed, though, because of our great jumping scores. As the jumps I was tackling got bigger, Mum would worry a little bit more with each show, especially after I had had some fairly nasty falls.

Mum found an amazing dressage and jumping instructor for me, who happened to be an international competitor. Her name was Cheryl and the way she encouraged me and calmly taught me how to focus helped Lady and me win many events. She would get on Lady to show me how she made her lengthen her stride; she would then show me how to time her strides to prepare for jumps. Because she showed me visually, I learnt first by what I was seeing, then by what I was hearing. By seeing it, then hearing it, then doing it, I learnt and remembered and never forgot. I now understand this is typical of a kinaesthetic learner.

Cheryl had the same gentle approach to teaching and tuning in with your horse as Liz from Kowhai. Both women had a profound impact on me. There was never any pressure from

39

them to learn, only encouragement. Over the years I had had some bad experiences with other instructors as they used to tell me what to do, or tell me how to do it, and when I didn't do it correctly they would tell me sharply that I had done it wrong, and so I lost a lot of confidence in myself. Both Liz and Cheryl empowered me with the belief that I would one day be a professional horsewoman like them.

When Lady came into my life we still lived on a normal-sized block of land, so we had to rent a paddock as we had done for Sandy. However, Lady's paddock was quite a bit further away than Sandy's had been. By car it was relatively close, but by pushbike, with a saddle across the handlebars, a bridle hanging from one handlebar and a bucket of feed hanging from the other, and hay strapped onto the back, pedalling into a headwind in the icy winters of Christchurch, it seemed to take forever to get there! None of that mattered, though. I just wanted to be with Lady as much as I could.

On my daily pushbike trips, I always rode past a very small paddock, which was home to a horse that seemed to be getting skinnier and skinnier each week. I was very worried about him as it was clear he was being neglected. Being indifferent to another being's suffering is to me the epitome of cruelty. It truly is one of the few things that makes me furious.

The house on the property had been rented to a big group of young men. There were many motorbikes and old cars scattered across the front yard, as well as evidence of some serious parties. The property had previously been a horse stud and it turned out that the abandoned horse had been an old teaser. Teasers are used in a stud to encourage the mares to be a little bit more obliging when it comes time to be served by a stallion. They give an indication to breeders when mares are ready to be served. Not all studs use teasers and it is a bit of a sad job for the horses as they are banished from any participation once the real stallion comes along. When the stud owners moved out, they apparently just left the horse behind because he wasn't important enough to be taken with them.

I used to sneak around the back of the property so that I wouldn't be seen by anyone in the house and smuggle food and treats to him. He was starting to recognise me and would always greet me with a nicker, which I was afraid would draw attention to me. The group of guys living in the house probably didn't even know how to look after a horse, so keeping the dirty bath filled with water was likely as far as they thought their responsibility went. I couldn't stand to see an animal kept in this condition and I was waiting for an opportunity to get him off the property without being seen.

One day I took a couple of horse rugs with me to cover him up so that he wouldn't be recognised as I led him down the road to safety. I snuck in through the back of the property when I was sure there was nobody there. I popped the rugs on him – he was so happy to see me, I'm sure he knew I was there to save him – then I proceeded to sneak him out the back gate, along the road behind trees and let him into one of the back paddocks where I kept Lady. Then I rang the RSPCA. They fined the old stud owner for abandonment and neglect and found my special rescue horse a happy home, where he was looked after and loved.

In my second year of high school, my mum had me apply for an alternative school, the first of its kind in our area. She did not want me to be subjected to another year of bullying, and I was still struggling with lessons. My new school was fantastic as it catered for students who were a little bit different and the teachers understood that we needed alternative ways of learning. The school was an old-fashioned two-storey house, and instead of desks we had beanbags. The Avon River and botanical gardens were at the end of the street, and we would regularly go canoeing and do our lessons under the trees in the gardens. Not being under pressure to learn helped my confidence greatly, but my brain still struggled dreadfully with maths and science.

My self-esteem was crushed when I couldn't even pass an English exam. I was so anxious beforehand as I had tried to study but could not focus on the words, so I went into the exam room a ball of nervous energy with no hope of concentrating. I felt such a failure. If it hadn't been for the confidence I felt competing in the show ring and working around animals, I don't know what I would have done.

The school supported and encouraged my love for horses and animals. They could see that I was most animated and happy when they asked me how Lady and I were going at shows, so they organised for me to do two days a week work experience in a veterinary clinic. So many of the alternative schools I now work with operate on the same principle: they find out what motivates their students so that they can find them work experience in that area. For me at that stage, all I wanted to do was work with animals.

When I was fifteen, the veterinary clinic offered me a full-time position, and Mum and Dad allowed me to leave school. The vets were really impressed by the way I cared for all of the animals before and after their surgery and with the time I took with the distressed owners when they brought their pets in to the clinic. The only problem was that I didn't cope very well with animals that had to be put down when no homes could be found for them. Often when my dad came to pick me up from work I would be standing in the car park with one animal or another, begging him to please take them home with us. Mum and Dad did actually take on quite a few of those abandoned animals, but I think I pushed the limits when I came out the door one day with two giant greyhounds. Seeing me, Dad just shook his head. So I had to turn around and take them back inside. I cried all the way home.

As well as Lady, I had an assortment of little dogs and cats and the odd bird that completed my animal family. I had two cats called Starsky and Hutch as that was the 'in' TV show. I got Starsky and Hutch when they were tiny kittens as their mum had been brought into the veterinary clinic after having been hit by a car. The kittens were delivered by caesarean and Mum and I fed them with a dropper until they were old enough to eat solid food. Mack was a little terrier-cross and he came everywhere with me. He was amazing with the kittens. He used to pick them up gently by their scruff and pop them back in their little bed and snuggle down with them. It was so beautiful to see him looking after them as if he were their mother. When I went riding on Lady, he would follow us everywhere. When he got tired, he would jump up and I would catch him and he would sit in front of the saddle and ride with me. He would sit up against my stomach with his little paws on each side of Lady's mane.

Somehow I always seemed to have adventures with animals in workplace situations. As well as working in the clinic, I was also helping out in a local boutique on my days off. Of course when I was working in the boutique I looked totally different to when I was riding or working in the paddock. It was a bit like playing dress-ups for me. Usually I was interested in making sure my horses were dressed nicely, with smart saddle blankets and gleaming tack; it made a change to be paying attention to how I was dressed for once.

One day a couple of girls came in and started trying on lots of different clothes. I was a bit suspicious of them, but in those days we didn't have anything like security cameras or electronic security tags. I was trying to watch them as closely as I could without being too obvious as, by the look of them, they would have become aggressive had they thought I was accusing them of shoplifting. When they left I double-checked everything and, to my horror, realised that two expensive designer jumpers were missing. I was devastated as I felt I had let the owner of the shop down. They must have put them on underneath the clothes they came in with. I was dreading ringing up the owner, but I did so and of course he was very disappointed and upset.

I just felt so bad. I went home, changed straight into my riding clothes and put my hair up into a ponytail. I greeted the little family of kittens that we had at the time but I'd accidentally left the front door open and, without me realising it, one of the kittens had wandered off outside. Someone was knocking at the front door and when I answered it I could not believe my eyes. It was the shoplifters, and they were wearing the stolen designer jumpers! One of them was holding my little kitten and asked, 'Is this yours?' Well, I tried to keep my face neutral, slumped my shoulders, changed my speech a little and said, 'Yeah, it is.' The second the door was shut, I raced to the phone, rang my boss and said, 'You won't believe what's just happened!' He said, 'Where are they now?' I told him it looked like they were heading down to the bus stop. He lived close by, so within a couple of minutes he had driven his car around to my house. I jumped in the back, slumped down in the seat and peeked over the window so I wouldn't be seen. I spotted them at the bus stop and he pulled over, and without them seeing me, he got his jumpers back. Who would have thought that my wandering kitten would have ended up being an undercover detective? I couldn't believe that they didn't recognise me, but I guess Paddock Sue looked quite different to Glam Sue!

CHAPTER 4

I still had Lady when I got married at eighteen. I met my first husband when I was seventeen and by nineteen I was expecting my first child. I was so excited to be having a baby. We lived very close to my mum and dad so we had lots of support. Towards the end of my pregnancy I had the help of a wonderful young girl I had met at pony club, who rode Lady for me. She was a fabulous rider and looked after Lady as though she were her own.

One day she was returning to the paddock when a car-load of young men drove past at high speed and threw empty beer bottles at her and Lady. Lady got such a fright she spun around and the girl was thrown off. Luckily she was unhurt, but Lady began galloping back to her paddock. As she was turning the corner, she was going so fast on the tarmac that she slipped and landed heavily on her hip. She managed to get back up and get herself home, and waited at the paddock gate until we got there.

We did not know the extent of her injuries until she went down that night and could not get back up. It is always dangerous when this happens because when horses are down for a long time the weight of their body can prevent blood flow to certain parts of their body, affecting their lungs and other organs and damaging nerves from the excessive pressure. We had vets attend her and we were told to roll her every few hours. They made a big sling and attached it to the rafters of the barn we had Lady in and tried to hoist her up into a standing position so that they could see how bad her injuries were. The trauma of that was horrific. As they were winching her up, the rope snapped and she fell back down. It must have been agony for her.

Her hip had totally collapsed. I was desperate to find a solution, to get her well again. It was an obsession. I couldn't sleep. I felt so helpless; it was all completely out of my control. My anxiety was at fever pitch. I just couldn't bear to see my beautiful Lady lying there and not being able to get up. The bond we had was so deep, my heart and soul felt like they were both breaking. All I was thinking when I looked into her eyes was, *I can't lose you, Lady, I just can't.*

I was sleeping in the stable with her every night, with her head in my arms. Every time I left, she would nicker, and then every time I returned she would neigh as loudly as she could. My whole family was concerned about the toll it was having on me as I was in the last month of my pregnancy and I had been nursing Lady for over a week.

A local paper ran a story on what had happened and the implications of those young men behaving in such an irresponsible way. A vet in charge of a big racehorse hospital on the other side of town saw the article and offered to try to treat Lady. The only problem was that we had to get her to his hospital. At the time there was a church being built across the road from our paddock. All the tradespeople working on that church offered to come over and help us to get Lady into an open, flat-bed trailer. They brought over a huge door and put metal rollers under it. We very gently rolled Lady onto a big ramp and slowly but surely moved that door until it was on the bed of the trailer. Then we packed hay and horse rugs all around her so that she was safe and comfortable. She was very calm and patient, as though she knew that everyone had come together to help her.

At the hospital they tried to winch her up in a sling so that the vet could have a good look at her injuries, but she was so exhausted he could see it was too stressful for her. He gently lowered her back down and said that he would try again tomorrow, when she had been rested. With his help, we made her as comfortable as we could in a straw-filled area and I prepared to snuggle down with her for the night. The vet told me that I needed to go home and get some sleep. Everyone said she was in good hands, that it was fine for me to go and come back first thing in the morning.

As I hadn't left her side for over a week it was terribly hard for me to leave. I went and sat with her and stroked her beautiful head and told her I loved her and that I would see her in the morning. I was so exhausted, I could hardly stand, but still, had the vet not insisted that I go home, I would have slept with her in the horse hospital. What happened next was amazing because she was so weak and exhausted. As I left the room, she lifted her head right up, swung it around towards me and let out the loudest neigh I'd heard since she went down. It was as if she knew she was saying goodbye to me.

The phone rang at six o'clock the next morning with the dreadful news that she had passed away during the night. Even though I understood that the chances of her becoming sound again were slim, I blamed myself for leaving her side that night.

The effect this had on me was profound. It was my first experience of death. I had never lost anything or anyone close to me. I could not understand how all that incredible energy that was Lady had gone. I cried for hours on end and my husband and family were very concerned. I could not seem to accept that this had happened to my beautiful Lady. One minute she was an amazing, powerful, strong horse, and the next she was reduced to helplessness. I felt anger at the boys who had caused the accident, guilt that I wasn't with her when it happened and that I didn't stay with her the night she died, and heart-wrenching sadness that she was gone. How could I ever have that depth of relationship or connection again? My dreams for her were over in the blink of an eye. My plan that she would have a foal one day so that I would always have a part of her with me was gone. Helplessness and depression engulfed me.

I was visiting my Uncle Bob, Dad's brother, and my Aunty Hazel one day not long after I had lost Lady and we were sitting in the lounge having afternoon tea. I remember trying to focus on our conversation but all I could think of was Lady. Uncle Bob explained to me that all of the incredible energy that was Lady had to have gone somewhere. We had such a great conversation. He made me aware of things that I had never been aware of before. He talked to me about the energy field that all living beings have: trees, plants, birds, animals; everything that's alive in the world. He explained to me that death is not the end, rather it's a transference of energy from one form to another. This made me aware that there is a living energy in everything around me and it made me start looking at the world in a different way.

Spirituality to me means appreciation of all the extraordinary creation we have around us. When you start to appreciate the wonder and beauty in the trees, the flowers, the ocean, the rivers, all the animals and birds and insects, it can make your soul sing, as you connect to the beautiful world of creation. I try to teach my students to be aware of the natural world; it helps them to stop looking inwards all the time and to start looking out. I have come to understand that the more you are connected to nature, the more empathy you have for all living things.

My conversation with Uncle Bob helped me find some peace and to focus back on the joy of the birth of my beautiful first child, Daniel, who arrived a few weeks after Lady's death. The joy and love I felt in becoming a mum was such a contrast to the grief I had been experiencing, and it helped heal some of the pain at losing a soul mate.

Lady has never ever left my heart, though, and the pain remained raw for many years. Even writing this has been incredibly difficult. Looking at her photos still brings me to tears as it stirs up so many emotions. My love for Lady has never diminished and I still miss her so much.

CHAPTER 5

We moved to the Gold Coast in 1981, when Daniel was three months old. My brother had moved to Queensland the year before with his wife and two young children. His stories of warm winters and beautiful beaches were too much for us to resist; besides, there were more employment opportunities in Australia. My sister was divorced by this time so she and her two children, Chelle and Amy, came with us. Pam later remarried and had a son, Andrew.

After losing Lady I was more open to moving away from the place that held so many bittersweet memories. Once in Australia, I realised that moving to a new country is more emotionally fraught than I had anticipated. For the first time in my life I was not surrounded by snow-capped mountains and pine forests. I had never lived in a city before and the freeways and highways were overwhelming. Surrounded by buildings rather than nature, I found my anxiety quickly reached a peak. I had never in my life been in a large shopping mall, and being in an enclosed building with no windows, glaring fluorescent lights and so many people made me yearn for the silence and emptiness of the pine forest. I have now learnt that shopping centres, with their overload of visual and auditory stimulation, are not a good mix for someone who is oversensitive and suffers anxiety. For the first time in my life I didn't have nature close at hand to soothe me when I felt overwhelmed and it made me realise how much I depended on it to keep me calm and balanced. Finding somewhere to live close to the water with some big open spaces for horses was my first priority.

I really didn't settle until Mum and Dad arrived. I had missed them terribly and this was the first time our family had been apart. Once we were reunited we didn't move far away from each other again, and we have remained living close ever since.

The fitness boom was just beginning in Australia and I was part of it from the very start. The fitness industry was a natural environment for me as it was motivating, positive and fun, and it wasn't long before I became an instructor. There were always child-minding facilities in the fitness centres so Daniel could come with me. It was lovely being at work and knowing he was just next door. To have a job that paid me to move was my ideal. I loved teaching aerobics, and being able to dance and sing through classes was such a relief as I could feel all of my energy being used in a positive way (as I used to do when I was showjumping with Lady), and being able to motivate and help others was a joy to me.

I soon realised I had a natural affinity for training people who struggled with self-image problems. I had always had an empathy for animals that weren't happy and I found my empathy was even stronger when I was working closely with unhappy people. I loved helping them change from having no confidence and low self-esteem to being proud of their fitness goals and regaining their confidence. I was particularly sensitive towards those who seemed so shy it was hard for them even to come through the gym door. Helping them feel as though they belonged was a pleasure, as I knew from my schooldays what it felt like not to fit in and I didn't like to see others feeling that way.

To obtain my fitness qualifications I had to attend TAFE college. I was incredibly stressed at the prospect of having to study and learn, but I found to my delight that I took to learning with a passion. I had a fabulous friend, Jill – we're still friends today – who had been a school teacher before she started in the fitness industry. She used to come over and help me study and she taught me how to learn anatomy to songs.

In my head I would sing through the body parts and that's how I remembered them. So having left school at fifteen without even being able to pass English, I was amazed to come through that course with Honours. I could not believe that I had passed subjects like physiology and anatomy when I couldn't even pronounce half of the names properly!

I thrived in the positive environment of the fitness industry. Back in the 1980s there was a strong sense of fun involved with getting fit. There didn't seem to be the same intensity about training as there is these days; there was certainly no such thing as bootcamp. It was all about fun and fitness, even down to the fluoro aerobic wear, headbands and matching leg warmers.

I even thrived on the energy it took to prepare classes. I had to practice my routines and update my music regularly (which in those days were on cassette tapes), so participants wouldn't get bored with the same songs. Even setting up for class would be busy – if I was teaching a circuit class it involved lugging in stationery bikes, weights and barbells from out of the gym to arrange around the aerobic room (and then having to put it all away after I finished the class). Without fail there would be a problem with my sound system, for example my tape would get caught in the cassette deck and I would have to run to reception to get a pen, standing there in front of the class winding the tape back into the cassette, while they waited, with their arms folded, for the class to start (sometimes up to 60 people). There would be days when

I would have my equipment all set up, my tape running smoothly in the tape deck but then the microphone batteries would go flat, so off to reception I would dash trying to pant out the words to the receptionist, 'quickly, quickly get me a fresh battery' before madly dashing back to the room to keep everyone moving. It was always constantly go, go, go – just what I loved. I thought it was perfectly normal to always be going one hundred miles an hour. I wondered why some other people didn't have the same energy that I seemed to have. At this stage I had no idea what my hyperactivity was, so I did not know any other way to be.

When Step Reebok was launched in Australia in 1991, I attended the training workshop and became hooked. I was running a little gym inside a medical centre at the time. I talked the director of the centre into ordering some step boxes as I wanted to start teaching classes as soon as possible. While we were waiting for delivery, I began practising the routines on one of the boxes the doctors used to help patients step up onto the examination table. They were quite suitable for doing basic moves on, so I decided to start running an Introduction to Step class straightaway. The amount of times doctors would come into the gym saying, 'Sue, give me my box back,' and I would say, 'But there's someone about to use it. Can't you use something else to get your patient up onto the table?' It was all done very light-heartedly as they understood my enthusiasm. It wasn't long before the real thing arrived.

I have photos of me stepping merrily away, just a few weeks before I gave birth to my second son, Jake.

Being part of the medical centre led me to help people with obesity. Those I helped often had low self-esteem and I had a great deal of empathy for them – I knew how that felt, and the way it often led to depression and anxiety. People wouldn't have known it then – if they'd met me they'd have seen someone brimming with energy and confidence – but I was experiencing very high highs and incredibly low lows.

When you suffer from constant anxiety (I didn't under-stand it was anxiety back then, I just thought it was excessive energy and that it was normal) and run on adrenaline as I did, your body exhausts itself. I was running on nervous energy, which meant I had stress hormones constantly pumping through my body. This is only meant to happen in an emergency so your body can quickly get to safety, but anxiety keeps your body constantly in flight or fight mode so at some stage you literally collapse with exhaustion. It was normal for me to go a hundred miles an hour and then crash, then back to a hundred miles an hour again and then crash. I never allowed myself to stay in the crash area for very long as my drive to exercise was so strong I could never rest properly. I didn't realise it at the time, but this was the beginning of an exercise addiction.

There is a fine line between being in control of your exercise and exercise controlling you. When exercise rules your life to the extent that it interferes with your relationships, social life and health, there is a problem. If I missed a day exercising I would be anxious, distracted and out of sorts. I would always volunteer to teach extra classes or to teach two or three classes back to back as it took that much exercise to take me to a point of feeling calm – or my version of being calm.

My competitive streak had surfaced when fitness competitions made their appearance in the late 1980s. I spent many years competing in aerobics competitions and then I started body-shaping competitions. Goodness, the work to get ready for those events! I took part in the mixed pairs aerobic competitions with one of my colleagues, Xen. He was a fitness fanatic too and we would rehearse our choreographed routine for hours. We once performed to 'Shadow Boxer' by the Angels. It really stood out as the other competitors were not using rock music back then! Xen and I often made the finals but as we didn't have gymnastic backgrounds like many of the other competitors, our inability to perform some of the more challenging moves, like leaping through the air and landing in the full splits, set us back a few points.

Being an aerobics competitor in those days was like being a full-time athlete because of the amount of training we did on top of teaching our usual classes. The body-shaping training was a different matter, as apart from weight training every day and doing aerobic exercise, we had to learn and practise a choreographed posing routine. The dietary requirements to get stage-ready, to obtain pure lean muscle, were exhausting as we were doing an incredible amount of exercise on a reduced calorie intake. Preparation of meals prior to competition required an exact balance of protein and carbohydrate and I would eat up to six meals a day but they were only very small. On competition day I'd be starving and dehydrated but if I won a trophy it made it all worthwhile!

My hard work began to pay off as I found myself getting quite a name in the fitness industry. However, there was a price to pay. I was pushing myself to my limit. Constantly competing, training and restricting what I ate was exhausting. When we went out as a family on weekends, I always had my own food packed in an esky and I would not allow myself to have any treats. This is a common way for competitive body builders to live, but nowadays there is so much more education about nutrition, rest and recovery, so there is less burnout and fewer injuries for those who train professionally. It never mattered how exhausted my body became, my hyperactive brain would always be dragging my poor body off to do more exercise. Friends and family all used to comment on how fit and motivated I was, so on the outside I seemed to be the epitome of health, but they had no idea what was going on with me mentally.

I was contacted by various fitness equipment manufacturers to promote their products. I also ran health and fitness shows to promote a healthy lifestyle. I staged regular shows at one of the Gold Coast's major shopping centres. I had a stage filled with fitness equipment to replicate a real gym. I had a little aerobics class going on in one corner, weight trainers using the equipment in another corner, and a cardio section with stationary bikes and treadmill. Most of the participants of my aerobics classes ended up being talked into being extras in my shows, and my mum and my sister were always in my displays somewhere on stage.

I organised fitness sessions for convention groups and got the name Super Sue Super Fitness. I was constantly booked to compere shows and events (even fashion shows – goodness knows how that happened), to promote local businesses and to appear on television and in infomercials. A local tourist park called Koala Town asked me to promote their organisation which, as well as koalas, had goats, birds, kangaroos and various other animals. The park was slightly off the beaten track, so I came up with the idea that if the tourists didn't come to Koala Town, we needed to take Koala Town to the tourists. I booked a big stage in the middle of Surfers Paradise, then I loaded a koala, a goat that did tricks with an accompanying clown, and a snake and his handler into a minibus and set up the Koala Town Stage Show. Everything was going brilliantly and it was time for me to announce Harry the Goat and his clown onto the stage. Up until now Harry had been perfectly behaved, standing backstage quietly, waiting for his moment. As Harry and his clown came on stage I was revving up the crowd, promising that they would see all sorts of amazing goat tricks. Harry stopped right in front of me in the middle of the stage, stretched his long hairy legs and did one of the longest wees I have ever seen a goat do! It seemed to go on and on and on. There was even steam! The crowd were open-mouthed, no doubt also amazed at how long Harry could pee for.

I was a regular motivational speaker at corporate conventions on the topics of health, positive thinking and self-motivation. I was very passionate about sharing my experience of being labelled as unable to learn at school yet going on to become very successful in my field. Being able to achieve your goals even when people doubt your ability is the epitome of self-motivation. I would run mini Ironman and Ironwoman competitions for convention participants, with silly cycle races and swims in the hotel pools.

I also had a team of actors and models for entertainment and exercise segments throughout the conventions to keep the delegates motivated and focused. A Sydney production company booked my services for the launch of a new Toyota motor vehicle which was staged at Jupiter's Casino on the Gold Coast. I organised a team of body builders, athletes and models and choreographed a routine to the song 'When The Going Gets Tough, The Tough Get Going', which was Toyota's theme song for that promotion. All this was all done in conjunction with running a fitness centre and competing. My hyperactive energy fuelled my active, action-packed days. I didn't know how to have a quiet, low-key job.

It was completely normal for me to be juggling several different jobs at once, as well as a busy home and family life. I loved the fact my job gave me the flexibility to cram everything in, but without my realising it, my nerves were starting to fray. My passion for wanting to do everything was beyond my body's capacity to handle. Being known locally as a so-called fitness celebrity, I felt enormous pressure to stay in peak condition, and this eventuated in my exercise addiction becoming full-blown. I felt I had to stay fit and lean so I was ready at any time to do a fitness promotion, television appearance or to teach a class to an A-grade sports team. It became such a way of life to me that I couldn't remember ever not exercising at this intensity. I was no longer driving the exercise; it was driving me.

Exercise addiction involves either purging yourself with intense exercise after eating or always needing the hit of endorphins, the feel-good chemicals that are produced in the body during intensive exercise. For some people it is the need to burn body fat, for others it is the need for the endorphin hit. For me it was both. Exercise gave me a great feeling as it seemed to work the anxiety out of my body so I felt relaxed after a huge session. In fact it wasn't really working out my anxiety, it was flattening it slightly, and what I thought was relaxation was actually exhaustion. In addition, even if I was exhausted I still had to push myself to burn off any extra food I had eaten.

There were times when I was exercising intensively for five hours a day. I used to teach back-to-back aerobics classes in the morning, return in the evening and teach another two classes, and then go for a run after dinner to make sure I had burnt enough calories. I was even training for a half marathon, which I ran two years in a row. No one realised that I had a problem. Certainly I didn't think there was anything wrong. I felt driven to exercise and I thought that was normal because it was the height of the fitness craze and everyone seemed to be frantically exercising. It felt like I was always going 100 miles an hour. The fact was I didn't know how to not go 100 miles an hour. I crammed in so many things I never wanted to miss – my sons' sport days, park time, fun – everything was packed in. I loved that my job gave me the flexibility to fit it all in but I didn't realise that my emotions were starting to get the better of me and my body couldn't handle everything I was trying to achieve.

Looking back I can see quite clearly that I needed a horse in my life. In the past that was how I had dealt with my anxiety, because looking after a horse always translated into having a horse to look after me. When I had any spare time I would go to a local equestrian centre for a trail ride, but this in no way compensated for having a horse of my own to connect with.

CHAPTER 6

At this time I had a great friend who was also completely horse mad and had the same quirky sense of humour as I did; she also happened to be a Kiwi. Janine and I had become quite attached to a couple of the horses we used to ride at the equestrian centre. One day she and I were there watching a rider doing some jump practice on a big black horse. I was quite horrified when I saw the fear on this horse's face as he was being asked to jump around the course. He knocked over many rails and refused many jumps. He looked terrified. His ears were back, his head was high, the whites of his eyes were showing and he was sweating profusely. When the rider was finished he rode over to where we were standing. I could see his frustration matched the horse's fear. I could sense something in this horse's eyes. He seemed lost, detached and anxious.

I felt very sad for him and I asked the man whether he was for sale. He said, 'You're welcome to him. You can have him for three hundred and fifty dollars.' I didn't think twice, I immediately agreed. So there I was again, back to having a horse while living in town and renting a paddock to keep him in. At least I didn't have to ride a bicycle to see him every day! Instead I drove out every morning and every night. His name was David. He was so affectionate and gentle and he had previously raced unsuccessfully.

Janine fully understood the changes that began happening in my relationship with David, especially the bond that was growing between us, and it meant a lot to me to have someone in my life who spoke the same horsey language. Every day David trusted me a little bit more. I never pushed him to do anything I didn't think he was emotionally ready to do. When he seemed frightened of trucks passing the paddock I would just stand under the tree with him as the trucks went by, until he learnt they weren't interested in him. I wanted David to feel safe with me, to know that at no time would I abuse the trust he was developing in me. I could see his confidence growing daily. One day I gently rode him towards a small jump, and much to my delight, he happily popped over it. I slid off him and gave him the biggest cuddle and scratch and told him how proud I was of him and what a good boy he was.

He looked very pleased with himself. Each week we would do a little bit of jump practice; I would never ask too much of him and would only ask him to jump when I felt he was confident. Our jumps soon got bigger and our little course got longer and when he completed an event-sized course, I leapt off his back, gave him a handful of carrots and let him know just how happy I was with him as I had really missed jumping.

The closeness and companionship we developed during this time was beautiful. I remember one day it was raining quite heavily and I ran across the paddock to shut a gate. I didn't realise David was running along behind me. When I stopped and turned around he did a bit of a jump and started running around with his tail in the air and I ran around with him, in the rain. He made it joyous. We were actually playing together. When I ran, he ran. When I stopped, he stopped. When I took a few steps backwards, he took a few steps backwards with me. It was as if we were dancing partners.

As his confidence had grown so much and our partnership was so strong, I thought I would enter a local showjumping event. It was absolutely fantastic because we won! Much to my delight, the man who had sold me David was also competing and he was amazed to see David jump so well. He too said, 'Gee, I shouldn't have sold him!' just like the previous owner of Lady had said to me so many years ago.

Around this time I decided to look for a dog to join our little family. I went to the pound as I wanted to give an animal a second chance. When I was walking down the rows of cages – so hard to do as you want to take all of them home – dogs big and small were barking and jumping up at their gates as if to say, 'Pick me, pick me!' There was one dog who was sitting quietly, leaning against the side of his cage. As I walked up and down, he watched me continuously. His eyes never left me. I kept being drawn to him. There was a silent plea in his eyes. I said to the lady who ran the pound, 'I think I would like to meet him properly.' She replied, 'His name's Mick, and he's been here so long he's actually our Dog of the Week, so he is free.' He was a collie-cross-Labrador and was so gentle and loving. Once I had decided he was the one for me, I popped him in the car and his eyes never left me the whole time I was driving home. He knew I was rescuing him.

Mick was the most devoted dog I have ever had. He slept by my bed and when I got up during the night to go to the bathroom, he would follow me. Many was the night I nearly tripped over him in the darkness! As with all of the animals I have had throughout my life, the connection I felt with him was strong. To feel such devotion and love from an animal is a precious gift.

Dad became unwell when I was twenty-eight and we were all absolutely devastated when he was diagnosed with bowel cancer at age seventy. He was told that he only had three months to live. None of us could accept this and it galvanised us into getting Dad to see naturopaths and healers. During this period I was on my own with Daniel as my husband and I had divorced. I just didn't know which way to turn or how to cope with seeing my dad deteriorate before my very eyes.

Dad was such a gentleman in every sense of the word. He was always there for us all, and he especially enjoyed checking our cars to make sure they were safe to drive. I would often be dashing out the door to go somewhere and Dad would have the bonnet up on my car, checking the water and oil. It is such thoughtful little gestures that I hold in my mind and my heart: his patience with me when I was little, his willingness to immerse himself fully in my horsey world, his love and respect for Mum. He was such a presence of calm stability to our whole family. The heartbreak and anguish of watching him slip away was indescribable. When he became so unwell he could no longer stay at home, the entire family moved into his hospital room with him. We didn't leave his side.

One morning I went out into the hospital kitchen to make my mum and sister a cup of tea and Dad slipped away. I couldn't believe that I wasn't in the room when it happened. The grief of losing Dad was so overwhelming it felt like my whole body was breaking. I could not imagine life without my beautiful father. As a family we were absolutely devastated.

David became my solace during this time. There were days when I would go down to the paddock and just hug him, and the tears would not stop flowing because I felt so helpless in the face of Dad's illness. There hadn't been anything any of us could do to keep him from suffering. It was absolutely devastating. David soaked up so many of my tears in his beautiful mane.

Before long I became unwell due to stress, which had caused my immune system to stop functioning properly. It was the grief of losing Dad, as well as still being very busy at work. My priority was supporting my son Daniel, who was nine, and trying to cope with the loss of his beloved granddad. Thankfully, we really pulled together as a family. We all spent as much time as we could with Mum as we all needed the comfort of each other. A close friend of mine offered to take David on, as she could see how stressful it was for me trying to manage his day-to-day care. She had a property in the hinterland and she loved doing dressage, so it wasn't long before a well-fed, happy David was gracing dressage arenas around the Gold Coast and doing very well. I was able to visit him regularly and still enjoy my special David cuddles. Knowing he had such a comfortable new home alleviated my worries about him, but I was still struggling to deal with Dad's loss.

Despite the fact I was constantly rundown and exhausted and I picked up every bug that was going around, my exercise addiction was as strong as ever. It didn't matter how unwell or exhausted I felt, I still had to fit in exercise. It was a few years of living with this addiction before I was made aware that I had a problem. As a regular guest speaker at local events, I often talked about self-esteem and body image, and one evening I was asked to speak at a local Eating Disorder Association meeting. Before I was due to stand up and speak, I sat and listened to what the group participants were sharing with one another. As they spoke I realised that I suffered from some of the same things they were talking about. They said things like, 'As soon as I have eaten something I shouldn't have, I have to go for a run straightaway,' or 'I make sure I count every single calorie I put in my mouth,' or 'I have to get on the scales two or three times a day to make sure I haven't put on any weight.' Hearing others talking about their excessive exercise and dieting behaviours made me see very clearly that I had a problem myself.

I got to know the psychologist who was running the group and she played a huge part in my recovery. I started seeing her for counselling on a regular basis and this was when I became conscious that I have a problem with anxiety. As my exercise decreased, my anxiety increased, and I understood that instead of using drugs or alcohol to self-medicate, I used exercise. Recovering from exercise addiction is incredibly hard, because the compulsive drive to exercise is overwhelming.

I kept a diary to make sure I did not go over the quota of exercise that was optimum for my health. I started to understand myself and my anxiety. When I was very young, the constant movement of play helped keep the anxiety under control. When I started school, it started bubbling to the surface because of the restrictions to my movement, but immersing myself in horses allowed my bottled-up energy to be released into something I absolutely loved and that gave me a sense of peace. I began to realise I was an incredibly sensitive person – it wasn't my imagination after all. I can clearly remember as a young child walking into a room and literally being able to feel the emotions of other people. I could pick up the slightest expression or movement in body language, which always kept me in a state of hyper vigilance. Slowly but surely I managed to reduce my hours of exercise and deal with the anxiety this caused.

Having gone through this journey I developed a program called HELP – Health Education Lifestyle Program. I wanted to educate women about how their bodies worked and why extreme eating and exercise behaviours were detrimental to their wellbeing. People read and then practise the most ridiculous and sometimes dangerous weight-loss advice. There were women who would wrap their bodies with cling film under their tracksuits and then participate in three aerobic classes in a row; one woman ate only eleven apples a day as in her mind each apple was a hundred calories and she was on an eleven hundred calories a day diet; others could never say no to anyone, so the only way they felt they had control over their life was to control their body. I wanted to educate women so that they didn't believe some of the ridiculous information out there that could permanently damage their health.

I realised that if people understood how their bodies worked, about the difference between muscle and fat and how if you excessively diet your body actually eats through its own muscle, it would help them change their thought patterns and become healthier, both physically and mentally. I used a lot of cartoon diagrams to teach people how fat was burned, how muscle was built and how to eat correctly to make sure that those things happened. I was asked to deliver the HELP program to many support groups, schools and sports clubs, and it gave a great sense of achievement to be able to use my struggle with exercise addiction to help others.

CHAPTER 7

In 1992 I remarried, and a year later I had my second son, Jake. I had met Craig at the gym and we shared the same interest in health and fitness, except he was crazy about cricket having been a top-grade player, and I was equally crazy about horses. We solved that nicely as when Craig was playing cricket I was off on a trail ride somewhere!

Jake was a huge baby. He was ten pounds when he was born, and when Daniel held him (so happily) for the first time, Jake look liked he was about three months old. After Jake's birth my anxiety started to reach new levels. Every time I put Jake into his cot and left the room, I was overcome with terror that something would happen to him. I checked on him constantly. This feeling of fear became so overwhelming that I had to see my doctor about it. He suggested that I hire a breathing monitor that strapped around Jake's chest and set off an alarm if he stopped breathing. Jake had that breathing alarm on until he was nearly two years old, but even with the monitor in place my fear was still overwhelming. As a result, my doctor referred me to a counsellor. It was during these counselling sessions that I began to understand what was happening. Without my realising it, I had linked the fact that both Dad and Lady had died when I left their side, and as a result I was petrified that as soon as I left Jake he, too, would die. My unresolved grief and anxiety were being transferred to my baby son. I know now that I should have attended grief counselling after Dad passed away. Understanding where the fear was coming from was a revelation to me and it enabled me to move forward without the overwhelming fear coming with me.

I was still guest speaking regularly, as well as running a fitness centre and teaching aerobics, when I was approached to present infomercials on Channel Ten's *The Morning Show*, promoting health and fitness products. I became known as the One Take Wonder as I was able to present an entire infomercial in one take. How I did that amazes me to this day!

I also started to do some work as an extra. Whenever a warrior woman was needed as an extra in movies or TV shows, I was called in. In one particular series, *Raw*, I turned up on set having washed and blow-dried my hair, thinking I would be playing a part like Zena, Warrior Princess. Much to my horror, when I was taken into make-up, they plastered oil and mud right through my clean, swishy hair. All traces of make-up were scrubbed off my face and dirt was streaked over it instead. *Well, I thought*, trying to stay positive, *I'm sure I'll be in some flattering costume like Zena wears.* But upon entering wardrobe, I was told to put on a rigid armour-like leather jacket, leather leggings and a huge pair of leather boots, and was handed an enormous sword I could hardly hold up. I was then ushered outside to stand against the wall where wet mud was thrown all over my outfit, body and hair. To get to the set I was crammed into an opened-back four-wheel drive with eight huge guys who were dressed like extras from *Braveheart*, with huge beards, scraggy hair, armour and swords. So much for my image of galloping towards camera on a white charger with my hair flying out behind me. Instead I was wielding a huge sword in fight scenes and crawling through a muddy paddock filled with cow pats. What a glamorous life in the movies!

At this time I was also personal trainer to a wonderful lady named Liz, an entrepreneur in the health industry. She asked me if I would be interested in promoting a new nutrition and exercise program her company was introducing to Australia. It was a fabulous program, so I started not only training instructors in how to implement the program in centres but also presenting at the company's conventions. One day I was presenting to a huge audience and I was particularly nervous because I had to speak about cellular nutrition. This in itself wasn't a problem as I knew my stuff back to front, but I had trouble pronouncing the anatomical and physiological terms. By the time I was called up to the stage, I was in quite a state. I got to the top step of the stage and then tripped and landed in the middle of the huge display of nutritional products, which flew everywhere, rolling off the stage and down into the audience! After the shock, I just burst out laughing, and then the audience caught the giggles, and from that moment on the presentation flowed beautifully, as it was the authentic me speaking and not the me trying to pretend to be someone I wasn't.

Even though I was very busy with a family and work, I made sure I still had time in my life for another horse. This one was called Socks. I was lucky enough to be able to keep him between our friends Mark and Carmel's and Liz's properties which was not too far from where we lived; while I was training with Liz, Socks could have his head in the window. It was heaven for me having my horse so close. It made me realise I was still yearning for a property so my horse could live with me and my family. Saturday afternoons became my special time with Socks because that was when we would go for long rides together. He had a beautiful quiet nature and we would often ride around bareback, just a halter and a rope, and wander down to the local creek. His favourite thing was standing belly deep in the water, splashing and flicking the water everywhere. He was such a good balance for me as my weeks were so hectic.

Sadly, it wasn't long before I had to find another home for Socks, as finding the time to travel out to see him daily was taking its toll. A lovely family with young daughters took him on. The two young girls bonded with Socks straightaway and he instantly became part of their family. I was able to visit him regularly but one morning I had a phone call with the dreadful news that Socks had passed away. It turned out that he had a growth in his stomach, which I had been totally unaware of, and it was as heart-breaking for me as it was for the family that had given him such a loving home.

It was 2001 and I had celebrated my fortieth birthday in March. Daniel was now twenty and Jake nine. We were living in Burleigh Heads, on the Gold Coast, and my HELP program had just been given the stamp of approval by the governing body of Fitness Australia, so I could educate instructors on how to recognise exercise addiction and eating disorders in their clients. In order to gain accreditation I had to travel up to Brisbane to present my program to the directors of Fitness Australia. I was so nervous. When I walked into the room, they were all sitting in a row looking very intimidating. They had a whiteboard ready for me and off I went. I was very self-conscious about delivering my program to such professional people as my workshop was filled with my hand-drawn cartoons on fat and muscle, with smiley faces drawn on tummies. But when I finished my presentation, they all applauded and said it was one of the best ways they had ever heard basic physiology explained, made easy to understand with humour. I was over the moon as I had been so nervous leading up to that presentation. They gave me an excellent write-up in their fitness magazine and I began receiving enquiries from instructors all over Australia about running the workshop in their area. And to cap everything off, I was given a Nike sponsorship for my contribution to the fitness industry.

The future was looking so good, then suddenly came the devastating diagnosis that I had early-stage breast cancer.

My family and everyone around me were as shocked as I was. Here I was, running a fitness centre, teaching fitness classes, seemingly the epitome of health; it just seemed unbelievable that I would have cancer.

I had been to the doctor for an unrelated issue and she had asked me if I had ever had a mammogram or ultrasound. I hadn't, so she sent me off to have both. The strange thing was that I didn't even have a lump. Something about the calcification that was visible in the ultrasound made her concerned, so she sent me off to see a breast cancer specialist. Much later, I said to her, 'How did you know? What made you send me for a mammogram?' And she said, 'I just had a feeling.'

It turned out that she had just lost a friend to breast cancer and was incredibly vigilant with every female patient who walked in her door.

We were planning a trip back to New Zealand and were due to leave the following weekend. At the end of a particularly busy day at the gym I was talking to one of my colleagues about my excitement about returning to New Zealand, when my phone rang. It was the specialist – he said he'd like me to go in to see him as soon as possible. Fear rose up in me and my heart began to pound. I just knew it wasn't good news. When I hung up from the call, my colleague could see that something was very wrong as I had gone from such excitement to absolute devastation within a few minutes.

We cancelled out trip to New Zealand and the following week Craig and I went to see the specialist. He told us that he was concerned about one of the ultrasound pictures and that I would need to have my breast biopsied. The biopsy was done in hospital and was very uncomfortable as they couldn't get the needle into exactly the spot they needed to. After a few hours I was getting distressed as it was becoming painful and my anxiety was sky-high. They decided that I would have to go into surgery so that they could do the biopsy thoroughly. By this time my anxiety was getting really bad. I just wanted to know what was going on.

Craig and I were called back into the specialist's rooms a few days after the surgery. We sat down and he said, 'I'm so sorry, but you've got early-stage breast cancer.' I sat there in disbelief, feeling as though I was outside my body. My heart was racing and I didn't know what to say. The surgeon recommended a lumpectomy to remove the cancerous calcification, followed by radiation treatment. That was when the thought of having a double mastectomy popped into my head and the decision was made. I didn't want to continually worry that there might be some cancerous cells left. The decision came to me so strongly that I knew it was the right thing to do. When you get such a strong gut feeling about something, it is usually telling you to honour it and examine it more closely. I had absolutely no doubt in my mind that this was what I wanted to do.

'Are you sure you want both breasts off?' the surgeon asked. 'Do you want to go away and think about it?'

I replied, 'I have nothing to think about. I'm absolutely certain that I want both breasts removed.' I felt enormous relief at having made this decision, and after the surgery I was told that they also found early cell changes in the tissue from the other breast – so it was a good job I followed my gut feeling.

Trying to deal with everyday life after a double mastectomy was a challenge. I couldn't lift my arms. I couldn't brush my hair, I had to have help getting dressed and I had to sleep propped up. My family were amazing during this time, as were my close friends. I just wanted to get back to normal as soon as possible, but I couldn't even drive a car. Going from being extremely active to not being able to do very much at all was really hard. The feeling of helplessness was a rude shock to me. I had taken the ability to move and stretch and lift so much for granted that I could hardly believe that my body wasn't able to do what I asked of it. I was a very impatient patient!

After I had recovered, I went through many months of breast reconstruction. A tissue expander had being inserted under the skin when they removed my breasts, and over a period of months it was filled with saline to stretch the skin enough to allow an implant to be inserted. This is done in day surgery, without anaesthetic, and the feeling of the pressure as the expander is filled makes you quite breathless for a few hours until you get used to it. It was during this time that my anxiety reached a new peak. I felt fearful all the time and I couldn't sleep. I had trouble falling asleep and then I would wake in the early hours of the morning and not be able to go back to sleep. I felt as though I was on high alert twenty-four hours a day. I went to see a naturopath and was prescribed some herbs to assist my body to relax. I also started seeing a counsellor again to help me process the fact that I had had cancer in my body. Even though it was an early detection, I was really struggling with the fact that it had happened to me. I was relatively young, I was extremely fit and always ate healthy food. It was the last thing I had ever expected to happen to me at that time of my life.

The cancer battles of two well-known Australians, Belinda Emmett and Jane McGrath, had a huge impact on me. I was in the early stages of my recovery from surgery and in a way they had been my breast cancer success stories. Craig actually hid the newspaper when the news of Belinda Emmett's passing was made known. He knew what an effect it would have on me.

Rationally I understood that my cancer had been caught early, but when you are told you have something cancerous in your body, the clinical difference between stages doesn't help you emotionally. The feeling of dread and fear is something that is very difficult to understand for those who have not been in this situation. This is why counselling is so important as it teaches you different coping mechanisms to deal with these fears and it provides a more encouraging and positive approach to deal with your disease.

After going through reconstruction and counselling I wanted to encourage other women who were experiencing the same thing. This has always been a strong coping mechanism for me. I truly believe that when you help others, you help yourself. You become what you teach; when you give, what you receive in turn helps with your healing. When I was being bullied, I wanted to make friends with other children being bullied to help them feel better. When I went through my exercise addiction, I developed the HELP program to assist others. So it was perfectly natural for me to tell my surgeon, 'If any other young women are diagnosed in your clinic and are having a double mastectomy and reconstruction, I'm more than happy to meet them and show them how I look now and how I'm feeling.' As a result I spent time with quite a few women who had received the same diagnosis, and it was great to show them how I looked and reassure them that they were very safe in the hands of our wonderful surgeon.

There was one particular woman who was only in her late thirties and was devastated that she had been advised to undergo a double mastectomy. She felt that she would be disfigured and lose her femininity and worth as a woman. I tried to reassure her that she was more than a pair of breasts, she was a beautiful young woman with a loving family. Rather than focus on one part of her body, she needed to focus on the whole of her body, the whole of her 'self'. In the end a pair of breasts do not represent who we are, and ultimately what is important is the essence of our soul, our heart and the people around us.

During my breast reconstruction, Craig suggested that we start to look for my dream acreage where I could see my own horse out of the window. He understood how hard it had been for me to find new homes for my beloved horses when my work commitments had had to take priority. He was also sure it would help with my anxiety as I had often spoken about how different I felt when I was around horses.

At the time we were living in Burleigh Heads, not far from the beach, and all the properties on acreage seemed out of our price range. We were getting discouraged as we didn't know how we would be able to afford to move. One day we were shown a beautiful property that was in the exact area we wanted, only twelve minutes from Burleigh Beach. It turned out that the lady who owned the property was looking for a house to live in at Burleigh, so she had a look at our place and was happy simply to swap houses. Yes, swap houses with no extra outlay, and I finally had my horse property!

While we were waiting for settlement, I started looking at advertisements for horses for sale. Even though I was still going through reconstruction, I just couldn't wait any longer. Strangely enough, though, I was drawn to an ad for two miniature ponies. I had never had miniature ponies in my life and was quite amazed at how much I wanted to go and see them. One was a tiny stallion called Riley who was only about thirty-four inches high, and the other was Mindy; she was a few inches higher but very, very round, and she looked much larger! When I first saw Mindy she seemed frightened and Riley seemed skittish. There were a lot of children playing loudly on the property, with motorbikes racing around all the time. After getting to know Riley and Mindy, I realised their sensitivity made them very nervous around so much loud activity. My heart went out to them and I said to their owner, 'I'll take both of them.' Craig said, '*Both?* I thought you were just coming here to buy one!'

The excitement of moving day was eclipsed by the excitement of Mindy and Riley being delivered to the property.

As a bonus, we discovered Mindy was pregnant and Riley was the dad-to-be! The two of them settled in beautifully. They loved hanging around the front door. Jake thought this was brilliant, and as far as he was concerned, Mindy was his pony. She loved laying her head on my shoulder while I rested, recuperating from surgery. Mindy was such a beautiful companion to me during that time. I couldn't walk out of the door without hearing her friendly nicker as she followed me everywhere I went around the garden. From hanging out washing to tidying up outside, Mindy was there with me every step of the way. Her permanent spot was at our front door with Riley, and visitors would have to squeeze past her to open the door as she wouldn't move. She used to run her lips up and down the security screen so that I would know she was there.

At one stage there was another miniature pony in a paddock up the road. He seemed quite lonely and the owner of the property invited Mindy to go into the paddock for a few weeks to keep the grass down and to keep his little fellow company. There were quite a few occasions where my neighbour would ring and say, 'We've just seen Mindy jump the fence and she's speeding up the road back towards your place.' She would end up skidding to a stop at the front door. Even though she had a nice pony for company and grass far lusher than in our front garden, she would much rather be at home with me. She always looked quite insulted when it was time to put her back in the paddock. She chose to sleep outside my bedroom window towards the end of her pregnancy, so I could keep an eye on her, as miniature ponies can often run into difficulty giving birth because they are so small. Towards the end she got so big she would groan loudly and I'd alert the whole house because I thought she was having the foal, but she was just so heavy and huge that she struggled to get up onto her feet.

One early morning I heard quite a loud bang against our garden shed. I jumped out of bed and rushed to the door to be greeted by an incredibly tiny black newborn foal. He was still covered in membrane and looked as surprised as I must have when we saw each other. We named him Yogi Bear as he was like a little bear. Mindy was a wonderful mum and we kept them in the back garden so they'd be safe from any local dogs while he was so small.

The vet suggested we put Riley, the stallion, into a separate paddock as sometimes stallions could hurt a newborn foal. So that he wouldn't be lonely, I popped him next door with our neighbour's horse. They seemed to get on okay over the fence but once Riley was in my neighbour's paddock, their horse attacked him. Riley was kicked so badly his back leg was broken in a couple of places. We took him up to a special horse hospital in Brisbane. As he was so small, we simply lifted him up and placed him in the horse float, stacking bales of straw around him to keep him stable. When we got to the hospital we carried him inside and the wonderful team there X-rayed him. They told us where the breaks were and that they could attempt to put pins in; however, those pins might not stay intact because ponies are so heavy relative to their size and this could possibly cause him a lot of pain. We had to make the heart-breaking decision to put our beautiful little Riley, who was so gentle and sweet, to sleep. Craig and I were absolutely devastated.

Seeing Mindy and Yogi together without Riley as part of their little family was heart-wrenching. Mindy and Riley had been very close and I knew she was missing him as much as I was. The funny thing with Yogi is that he has exactly the same habits as Riley. Riley used to love undoing shoelaces, zips, gates and ropes that were tied to the fence, and Yogi has the same skills! Yogi can open gates that are meant to be pony-proof. He can slide open bolts on shed doors; he's even lifted gates off their hinges with his fat brown bottom and escaped that way. His habits when he was very young and still lived around the house ranged from stealing our shoes from the patio and flinging them into a nearby gully, to pulling the washing off the line and even jumping into our little above-ground swimming pool and having a wonderful time splashing around while his poor mum Mindy ran frantically around the pool, neighing and wondering how to get him out.

Every time I would start to get upset about Riley, Yogi would perform one of his talented acts. It was very strange. There would be times when I was feeling very low and little Yogi would pop up out of nowhere and do something to make me laugh. Little did I know that it would be Yogi's cheeky and adventurous personality that would melt the hearts of a lot of the angry and defensive young people who would eventually participate in my Horses Helping Humans™ program. Just as Mindy's gentle nature would give so much love and affection to young people who have never experienced that in their lives.

My reconstruction was going well. The couple who owned the gym where I worked were absolutely fantastic in their support of me. Returning to work with their encouragement and understanding played a huge part in making me feel that I was getting back to some kind of normality. I was working part time and running self-esteem and body-image workshops through my HELP program. I would usually be teaching an aerobics class in the morning or giving a personal training session, teaching my workshops either in the evening or on Saturday morning, and spending the rest of my time with my horses and with my family too. Now I was becoming so busy again, my anxiety was increasing. In my riding I had gone from being a successful, brave jumper to being anxious about even stepping over a rail on the ground, and that was a good analogy of how I was feeling in the rest of my life too. Anxiety makes you fearful of just about everything.

I have been asked by people who have never experienced anxiety what it feels like. I say it's like the feeling you have when you're walking down a dark alley and you think someone is sneaking up behind you. I felt like that all the time. The famous painting *The Scream* by Edvard Munch portrays anxiety perfectly. The first time I saw that painting, I thought, *Oh my goodness, the person who painted that knows what anxiety feels like!* There is an overwhelming feeling of fear and you just don't know where it's coming from. It robs you of confidence and self-esteem and makes you think that you can't achieve anything any more.

At times anxiety can sneak up on you with as much stealth as a ninja. It seems to appear from nowhere and strike. And as usual I was ignoring the warning signs that it was getting out of control by making myself busier and busier.

CHAPTER 8

I was still searching for a riding horse and I found a majestic thoroughbred called Scooby. When I first saw him being ridden he reminded me of Lady because of the way he held himself and the way he moved. Unlike Lady, though, he was quite nervy. He would jump even when a leaf fell from a tree. Of course, with a rider who suffered from anxiety, this was not a good match! One day when we were riding home through the park, a dog ran out from some trees, barking very aggressively. Scooby spun around, I was nearly flung off but just managed to hang on, and he took off at great speed, bolting across the whole length of the very large park. I have never gone that fast on a horse in my life. By the time I pulled him up, both his anxiety and mine were at fever pitch. A little bit more of my nerve was lost. I hadn't started Natural Horsemanship at this stage. I so wished I had, because it would have helped me train Scooby out of all of his fears. As it was, I felt in such a fragile state myself that I was quite helpless as to what to do with either of us.

A local woman purchased him as she wanted to do only dressage with him. She looked up his brand and discovered that his racing name had been Passmore and that he had won the Silver Slipper in 1999. No wonder he was so fast when he bolted that day! My surgeon would have been horrified if he'd seen that; I was still undergoing reconstructive surgery and I'd been told to go home and rest, not to be riding ex-racehorses at an uncontrolled gallop across parks.

I began to realise that a highly strung horse was not a great choice for me because of my anxiety levels and because I had lost so much of my nerve, so I began travelling all over the place to find a quieter horse. One weekend I went with my friend, Chris, to Uki, a sleepy little town in northern New South Wales. This was the first time I laid eyes on my amazing horse Sunny, who has helped me create Horses Helping Humans™, the highly successful program I run today.

The first time I saw Sunny, I said to Chris, 'No, I don't think he's the horse for me.' He was fairly short and his mane had been cut off so it stuck up and he looked quite punky. I'd always been used to riding big strong thoroughbreds and

I just couldn't imagine riding Sunny, a smaller quarter horse with a very short back and short legs and muscly hindquarters. He didn't look at all interested in being ridden or socialising, but I took him for a ride up the road anyway. We had driven all the way out there so I thought it wouldn't hurt to see what he was like. Well, he wasn't very enthusiastic about moving until we turned around to head back to the paddock. So it was lots of 'Go, go, go,' to get him to leave the paddock and lots of 'Whoa, whoa, whoa', when heading back to the paddock. He was really keen to get back to his paddock mate, a big old Brahman bull. The Brahman was monopolising all of Chris's time and attention as he wanted his head scratched and his face stroked. If I could have brought him home too, I would have.

After I got back from our 'Go, go, whoa, whoa' ride I said to the owner, who had bought Sunny for his daughter a few months previously, 'Could I think about it?' as I still wasn't convinced that Sunny was the horse for me.

I spent another week looking at other horses but Sunny stayed in my mind. I had no idea why. My friend suggested we go down and have another look at him, and I took him for another ride. When I got back to the paddock I was still umming and ahhing and the owner said, 'Look, just take him for a month. Try him out and if you're not happy, bring him back, and if you are, just send me a cheque.' So I brought him home and started to get to know him.

I distinctly remember the first time I took Sunny out for a ride down the road. Everything went well until we got to the end of the street and it was time to turn either left or right. Sunny would do neither. He planted his feet and refused to move. Obviously he'd gotten away with this in the past and he was so used to turning around and going home when he wanted. There we were, at the end of the street, and neither of us was budging. I was determined he was going to walk forward. He was determined to turn around and go home. I continued asking him to move forward. After asking him to move for ten minutes without any response, I was getting very frustrated and the anxiety was starting to kick in. I had to make sure he knew that I would not give up. So I kept going. I asked him to move forward; I flicked the reins against the saddle to create some energy and noise; I reached behind me and tapped his hindquarters; I tried to encourage him with my whole body to move forward – all to no avail. It was becoming exhausting but I knew, no matter what, that I could not give up.

There was no point getting angry as respect can't grow in anger, so I had to keep my anxious frustration at a very low level and overcome those emotions with calm determination. I think I'd been asking him to go forward for about twenty minutes when he finally turned his head around and looked up at me. He was realising that I was not going to give up. That was when our relationship started. After looking at me for a good few seconds, he turned his head to face front again and continued walking down the road where I wanted him to go. This issue never came up with us again.

Sunny became a hit with the whole family as he had this 'cool dude' attitude going. Nothing fazed him. Loud unexpected noises or trucks racing past us when we were out on rides never disturbed him. He always had a 'whatever' attitude, exactly what I needed to replicate in myself after being so anxious for so long. He was starting to help me regain my confidence as he never did anything to make me feel unsettled. Even if I was having a struggle with anxiety some days, he was never affected by it, he just calmly and happily carried me around the neighbourhood as if he had all the time in the world.

After losing Riley in the awful way we had, I was petrified that Sunny might hurt Mindy or Yogi, so we went to great trouble to segregate our paddock – there was always a fence between them. Yogi was growing into quite a cocky little man by then and seemed determined to connect with Sunny. He would strain his head through the fence, trying to grab Sunny by the tail or by his horse rug. Sunny would lean over the fence and nuzzle Yogi as a mare does to her foal. When Yogi was out of his sight, Sunny would become distressed, and as soon as Yogi was back in sight, Sunny would settle down. This gave me the reassurance that if I let Sunny in the same paddock, he would not harm Yogi.

The first time Sunny and Yogi got together, it was amazing. Yogi was absolutely beside himself that his big new friend was allowed to play with him. He went up on his back legs, with his little front legs waving towards Sunny. Sunny dropped down onto his front knees to make himself the same height as Yogi, so that they could neck wrestle. Mindy and I were watching together with amazement as I'm sure she had been as concerned as I was about putting the two together. From that day on, Sunny and Yogi have been inseparable. I always know when Yogi has done an escape job during the night, as the whole neighbourhood will hear Sunny screaming for his best mate to come home quick smart.

Sunny is a horse with a strong personality, and he always felt he knew how to do things better than I did. In some cases he did! For instance, when I first got Sunny I didn't know he was a whiz at opening gates. The first time I tried to open the gate without dismounting I had him facing the gate with me leaning over his head practically hanging from his neck, trying to unlatch the gate. On the next occasion he turned his head and looked at me and his expression honestly was 'For goodness sake!' He then turned himself so that he was alongside the gate and then backed us up so I was exactly level with the latch, allowing me to undo it easily. Once I had unlatched it he calmly walked sideways to push the gate open and then turned nimbly around to the other side of the gate and walk sideways to push it shut behind him, then moved forward into the perfect position for me to re-latch the gate. This became my party piece! I would offer to open and shut every gate when I was out with other people on trail rides, so that they could all see his awesome gate technique.

One day, when we were riding with friends through a big cattle property, he showed me that he thought he could do another job without me. We were riding through a herd of grazing cattle and, as we rode through, one of them bolted off to the side. Sunny spun around so quickly that I nearly fell off, in his enthusiasm to chase after the rogue steer and we nimbly steered him back towards the herd. I just couldn't believe what a quick-thinking worker Sunny was.

When I purchased Sunny I didn't know his origins; it was his gate technique that led me to the story of his past. I was attending a horsemanship camp at Cabarita Beach in northern New South Wales. In our free time, we took our horses to the beach, which was directly across the road from the camp. There was a big group of us and on the first day, as we approached the gate leading off the property, Sunny and I were in front so I could show off his gate-opening skills. A gentleman who was dropping off a horse went to open the gate for us. I called out, 'No, it's fine. I want to show all the others how impressive Sunny's gate skills are.' He stepped back, smiling, watched and then said, 'Hang on a minute, that's my old horse Decker.'

He recognised the white mark on Sunny's rump; apparently Sunny had cut himself when he was very young and it had grown back white. It was due to this white mark that the people I bought him off thought he was a half quarter horse, half Appaloosa. It turned out that the man had bred Sunny himself, and he was pure quarter horse. He said he was one of the smartest horses he had ever owned. He had sold him because he used to compete in camp drafting and Sunny thought he could round up the cows better than his rider so he was hard to check (that is, to slow down at the stipulated times). This all made sense of Sunny's 'get the job done' nature. It also made me realise why I had had such a struggle with Sunny at first. Even this strong cowboy who had bred him had struggled to show him who was in charge; no wonder Sunny hadn't liked me challenging his decision-making!

CHAPTER 9

I had had Sunny for around six months when I saw my first Natural Horsemanship demonstration. It took place in a big covered arena in Brisbane and was given by a very well-known Natural Horseman from America, Pat Parelli. Quite a few horses and handlers were in the arena practising their ground skills. None of us in the audience could believe what we were seeing. Horses and their owners were communicating and connecting without any halters or ropes. The owners were asking their horses to back up, to come back, to circle them, to pop over jumps, to run around the whole arena and then to return to them – simply by using their energy and body language. At one point all the owners turned their horses loose to run around the arena altogether. There were about eight horses running the full length of this huge indoor space. The owners then started calling in their horses, and even with all the high energy of the horses running around, and eight different people standing in the middle of the arena, each horse went directly back to its owner.

It was a moving and life-changing experience for me. I had had an inkling of this sort of connection with Lady but never to the extent of what I saw that day. The connection I had always felt with horses was being displayed at an amazing level. The relationship between the horses and their owners was so obviously based in trust and respect. Everything they were doing was what I had dreamed of being able to do since I was young. I couldn't wait to start learning more.

I immediately enrolled in the next Pat Parelli clinic, and so began my journey with Natural Horsemanship. Natural Horsemanship has been used by horsemen and horsewomen in the USA for many, many years. They have always known what beautiful spirits horses are, and how sensitive they are emotionally. Remarkable horsemen like Ray Hunt, Tom and Bill Dorrance, Buck Brannaman and many others, like Monty Roberts. In Australia, we now have some amazing top horsemen, who run many clinics for people to learn these wonderful techniques. They have brought the world of Natural Horsemanship into the public eye. They have shown people a different way to connect with horses, not to 'break' in a horse with fear and pressure, but to 'start' a horse with trust and respect. They encourage people to learn the language of horses, how they think, how they perceive the world around them, how they interact with one another. They show you how to ride with softness of hands and body so you have a freely moving, comfortable, confident horse. Finally, I would enter a world where you could talk to your horse through body language and energy.

In Australia, Ken Faulkner is a leading practitioner of Natural Horsemanship. When I met Ken, his teaching style resonated with me immediately as he has such a wonderful sense of humour, and he breaks things down so that they are easy to understand. I was like a sponge. I wanted to absorb everything. I attended Horsemanship clinics, camping with Sunny for up to a week at a time, which reminded me of my wonderful time at pony camp when I was younger. I felt I was living the dream all over again, days with just my horse and an amazing teacher. At one stage I carried a little notebook in my pocket so that I could write down all the wisdom Ken was sharing, but writing on a moving horse meant I couldn't understand half my notes!

Watching Ken working with difficult horses for a very short period of time and getting incredible results made me understand the effects of patient reinforcement. I have seen Ken working with dominant and aggressive horses, yet by staying calmly assertive as he is re-educating them, he builds respect very quickly. With nervous horses, the ones that often come across as flighty and unpredictable because they do not under-stand what is required of them, Ken builds confidence by never confusing them by getting emotional.

The relationship starts well before you saddle up. You develop trust and respect through many different exercises on the ground with just a halter and rope. This develops such a bond with your horse that it is as though you're dancing together.

One of the exercises is learning how to back your horse out of your personal space. Sunny and I demonstrated our mastery of this one day in quite an impressive way. A friend and I had travelled inland from the coast with our horses to meet another horsey friend for a ride in the cane fields and adjoining forest. Our friend's farrier was just leaving as I was unloading Sunny from the float. He said, 'I recognise that horse. I used to see him at camp drafting and rodeo competitions. It used to take quite a few guys to get him to back into the holding pen.' (The holding pen is a small starting enclosure used in some of the events.) I said, 'Yes, that sounds like the old Sunny, but watch this!' I held my hand up in front of me and simply moved my index finger back and forward. Sunny calmly backed into the chute (we had been to quite a few Horsemanship clinics by this stage). The farrier was absolutely gobsmacked.

Once we had mastered the ground exercises and were ready to jump on and ride, our bridles were taken off us in a safely contained arena and we had to learn to connect and ride with just a halter and a rope, no bits in the horse's mouths. It was like learning to ride all over again. This teaches you not to hang off a horse's mouth when you are riding but to use your whole body in a relaxed way. It teaches you how to make your horse soft and receptive. Imagine if you were a horse and someone was sitting on your back rigid and uptight, with either anxious or frustrated energy; you'd feel pretty tense and uncertain. When the rider completely relaxes and all that tension is released, it is such a relief to the horse and the two of you can start moving in sympathy with one another. Only after being able to work our horse safely and softly in a halter were we allowed to put a bridle back on. Even so, we were instructed that our hands always had to be very soft on the reins; because you are riding with your whole body, your horse can feel what you want them to do without you tugging and pulling on their mouths.

Over the years I had been filled with horror at seeing people ride with 'heavy hands', pulling so hard on the reins it can make a horse's mouth bleed, or kicking them hard and hitting them with sticks. To be in a world where the lightest of touch through your hands or body tells your horse what you want them to do was like coming home as that's all I had ever had to do with Lady. I felt I was finally regaining what I had lost when Lady died. It was possible to have that deeper level of connection again with other horses because here were people teaching it. I was finally around people who felt like I did. It made me realise just how blessed I had been to have riding mentors like Liz from Kowhai Pony Camp and Cheryl. It wasn't until I started having lessons with other riding instructors that I realised not everyone was as gentle and caring towards horses and taught their students how to ride them without force and aggression.

Natural Horsemanship is all about letting the energy flow naturally, not trying to hold it all under control. I distinctly remember one clinic with Ken Faulkner when Sunny was being exceptionally excitable. Everyone else was cantering their horses around, nice and relaxed, but Sunny just wanted to go. I was trying to hold him back but not feeling very confident. When Sunny gets overexcited there is a lot of energy going on! I remember Ken yelling out, 'Stop hanging on to that horse so tight. Let that energy go!' He wanted me to loosen my reins and let Sunny move. Well, move he did. But it wasn't long before all that bottled-up energy became relaxed and loose. It was a turning point for me, as I had to let go and trust. You would have thought that it would have made my anxiety worse, but it was actually liberating and it was the most free I had felt on a horse for many years. A term that Ken uses that I love is, 'Ride him like you've stolen him!' This describes perfectly that episode: Sunny was fighting me to go and I was fighting him to stay, but when I let it all go and drove that energy forward, it wasn't long before Sunny was asking me to slow down. What a turning of the tables!

It is important not to put too much pressure on your horse. When people expect too much and become impatient and frustrated, it builds resistance in the horse. For example, if you have a horse who is nervous about crossing water, rather than keep pushing him, encourage him to take the time to drop his head and look at the water, touch it with his foot and take it slowly in his own time. This will build up his confidence and help with his fear of crossing water in the future. Trying to force an issue only creates stress for your horse; when their environment is calm they become more confident. More doors of communication are opened when you learn to retreat (take the pressure off) than when you advance (put the pressure on) as this often simply slams the doors of communication firmly shut. And this is as true for humans as it is for horses. You never tell your horse what to do, you ask them (a lot of humans could do with learning this technique). And when your horse questions you or challenges you, always calmly and assertively reinforce what you are asking for without ever getting mad or sad. To earn Sunny's respect I had to always softly stand my ground so he came to understand that I never gave up, no matter how much he pushed me to stop when he didn't want to learn something new.

There were many challenging moments when I started Natural Horsemanship. I began attending clinics on a regular basis, travelling wherever I needed to, as I just wanted to learn so much. At first when I asked Sunny to circle me on a twelve-foot rope at the trot, he would either start racing around and around or not move at all. Finding that balance of energy between us took hours of practice. Teaching him to back away for me and step out of my personal space could be confronting as he just wouldn't budge. Patience and not getting emotional was a challenge for me at the best of times. Sunny's naturally strong personality felt intimidating to me at the beginning. Once I learnt the correct way to request things of him I finally got his full respect. When a horse respects you, they focus on you, they drop their head, they lick their lips – these are all signs that they are engaging with you. It was the best feeling and it made me realise that I wanted to feel respected in my human interactions in the same way.

One of Sunny's best friends is Max, a beautiful quarter horse-cross-Andalusian. He belongs to my good friend Chris and we have attended many horse clinics together. Chris and I would be chatting away nonstop all the way to the camp, with Max and Sunny in the horse float, looking like they were also chatting away with one another.

When you attend Horsemanship clinics you have to be absolutely dedicated, as no matter what sort of weather hits, you're still out there with your horse, learning. Flooded campsites, cyclonic winds, searing heat, none of it would stop us. Sometimes the worst conditions led to the most memorable camps. Chris and I always had additional adventures: flat tyres, leaking tents and general mayhem (it amazes me how some people can have organised, drama-free trips). At one camp we had been working with the horses all day in wet weather and by the time we had finished for the day I was utterly exhausted. I'm not a good sleeper but that night I was in one of the deepest sleeps I could ever remember. I thought I could hear my name being called in a dream but it was actually Chris outside in the pouring rain in her pyjamas and gumboots, desperately trying to wake me up as Sunny had escaped his yard and was running from mare to mare, revving them up, encouraging all the squealing, kicking out and general horsey flirting that a rig will cause. A rig is a horse that hasn't been castrated properly and he still has all the characteristics of a stallion. The noise woke the whole camp as it sounded like horsey chaos, so I'm sure they all thoroughly enjoyed seeing me slipping and sliding in the dark, in the pouring rain in my pyjamas and gumboots, trying to catch Sunny, who was enjoying being 'out with the girls' way too much.

The relationship between Sunny and I strengthened, but I also began noticing changes in myself. The foundations of Natural Horsemanship are trust, respect and patience and these attributes were having an impact on my anxiety. I was becoming calmer, more confident, and finding it easier to set boundaries in my life. In the past, I had always had a problem saying no. For as long as I could remember I had always put something or someone else's needs before my own, even to the detriment of my health. I would do things for others even when I was absolutely exhausted. It made me realise that to regain my health and emotional stability I had to start setting aside time just for me (and my horse!).

Everyone in my life seemed to be noticing the positive changes that Natural Horsemanship was bringing me. There was one striking example of this. I was competing in a Natural Horsemanship show in which you run into the arena with your horse at your side (at liberty, no ropes attached), and both you and your horse must come to a stop at a designated point. You are then asked to perform different tasks such as standing in front of your horse and getting him to back ten paces away from you and then asking him to come back in towards you using only your energy and body language. You are asked to circle your horse around, then change direction and circle back the other way, ask them to pop over a jump and finally, leave the arena with your horse's nose at your shoulder. On this particular day there was a mare in season on the other side of the arena. Every time we would start a new task, Sunny would get distracted by the mare and gallop over to her. I had to calmly get his attention back and request that he complete the task. It took me twice as long to get around that course than anyone else, but the end result was that he followed me out of the area with his nose on my shoulder, exactly as he was supposed to. At no time had I showed any frustration or anxiety, as I would have completely lost his respect and connection.

Much to my surprise, at the end of the day I was awarded Savvy Champion of the show for my ability to reconnect with Sunny, no matter what happened. Isn't that what we want in our human relationships as well, that no matter what happens we have the ability to reconnect when things go wrong?

One of the ladies at the show had not seen me for a couple of years. I knew her through the Horsemanship circle and we had discovered that we both suffered from anxiety. She had to take Valium when it got really bad, but as I get side-effects with just about any medication, I relied on herbs from a naturopath. On the day she saw me presented with my Savvy Champion trophy, she came over and whispered to me, 'Oh my gosh, Sue, you were amazing out there. You were so calm and centred.' And then she said the words that made my day: 'Are you on Valium?' I was absolutely wrapped! That proved to me how much I had changed, how much my new inner calmness was showing.

Sitting around the campfire at horse clinics, sharing our progress with each other, it was quite apparent that I wasn't the only one changing because of the experience of Natural Horsemanship. There were stories of fathers relating better to their wives and children, women learning to say no and to be more assertive, and young people gaining confidence, all in a relatively short period of time. My brain started ticking over, wondering how I could share all of this with people who didn't have a horse. It didn't seem fair to me that just because you didn't own a horse you should miss out on learning these amazing life skills. Without my realising it, the Horses Helping Humans™ Program was developing in my mind. How could I present these skills to people who had never ridden a horse in their life? How could I get all of this across in a short period of time so that 'unhorsey' people would walk away with a new awareness about communication with their family, friends and colleagues? There had to be a way, I just had to find it.

CHAPTER 10

In between my horsemanship clinics I had private sessions with an amazing horsewoman, Eliza Pridde. Eliza had been involved with Pat Parelli at a high level for many years and travelled extensively teaching and mentoring. She started her own Horsemanship clinics called Savvy Success. She would come every week and work with Sunny and me to get us through all of the tasks of Natural Horsemanship. Eliza found a way to relate to me with patience and directness so that I managed to retain everything she taught me. She understood me and did not make me feel inadequate when it took me a while to grasp things. She would explain it in different ways until I understood.

Her patience at that time was quite remarkable as she didn't know she was trying to teach someone who is a kinaesthetic learner. For me to learn, I have to see, do, see, do, see, do, until I get it. And being able to move around while I'm learning helps me to retain information. I have a habit of fluffing about while things are being explained to me, as it is very hard for me to stand still and just focus on words; at times this has been frustrating for people teaching me because they think I'm not listening. The truth is, if I try to stay still and just listen, I actually lose concentration and don't hear much at all. When I'm moving around, getting a drink or getting a snack out of my saddlebag, I'm actually hearing everything that is being said to me.

One day I was riding and practising backing Sunny up by literally holding my tummy in and wiggling my toes a little, without even touching the reins. On this particular day he wasn't listening to me at all. In fact, he kept going forward and trying to knock me into an overhanging tree! I was saying to Eliza, 'Why is he doing this? He did it perfectly last week.' She said to me, 'It's because you're not consistent on a daily basis. He's lost respect for your ask.' As I rode home from my lesson I began thinking about what she had said, and I realised it wasn't just with Sunny that I had a problem being consistent about my boundaries and goals, it was throughout my whole life. I clearly saw that things in the past that I could have made really successful had fallen by the wayside due to my inconsistency. Over the years I had come up with many great ideas, especially in relation to fitness programs. I would get an idea and then start putting something together to make it happen, but then I'd get caught up in something else and the great idea would be buried under the pile of other things I was trying to deal with at the same time.

This awareness could not have come at a better time as I was just beginning to develop the idea of the Horses Helping Humans™ program. Had I not been aware of my habit of being inconsistent, I don't believe the program would have reached the success it has today. Understanding that I tend to jump from one thing to another made me realise I had to stay absolutely focused if I wanted to make my vision happen. This wasn't easy. I had to create some sort of structure for the program, the very thing that had always challenged me even when I was at school. It was all very well to have the ideas and visions in my head, but to get them down on paper and transform them from ideas into a strong, results-based program required me to be as capable, competent and focused as possible.

I felt that the vision had committed to me so I then had to commit to the vision.

Once I started to apply this consistency to all of my sessions with Sunny, our relationship stepped up a whole level. No matter how I felt on different days – tired, anxious, boiling hot or freezing – I asked him to do things with the same calm, consistent and gently assertive energy. Problems arise in horse and human relationships when you are not consistent in your boundaries. You may express that something is absolutely unacceptable one day, but the next day if you're tired or feeling a bit lazy and don't stand by your decision, your energy and body language give the signal that it doesn't really matter. This creates inconsistency in your communication and leads to confusion in relationships as people (and horses) are not quite sure where you stand. Clear, calm decisiveness every time gives the best result.

It wasn't long before I could take all ropes and halters off Sunny and work with him at liberty. I felt an enormous sense of achievement at being able to do this as it had been such a challenge for me in the beginning. I remember the first day I started working with Sunny at liberty around the yard, he began running around me as I tried to bring him down to a walk using my energy. He started running faster and faster, which was making me extremely frustrated, so of course he started going even faster. My instructor came over and leant on the fence and simply said, 'Gee whiz, you've got a lot going on inside of you!' I replied, 'I'm perfectly relaxed, he's just not listening to me.' I did not at that point realise that it was my energy that was making him go faster. My instructor said to me, 'You've just got to focus on being calm and still and that is what Sunny will feel. Don't focus on all the other emotions you're experiencing.' You can imagine how fast Sunny was going at this stage as he was faced, at that time, with an owner who suffered bad anxiety.

I focused on Sunny and I breathed out completely, which dropped my energy very low, and all I thought was, 'Walk, just walk.' I found myself going into a meditative state as I was continually breathing out completely and focusing on 'Walk, slowly.' Much to my surprise at the time, Sunny's energy dropped and he settled into a nice quiet walk around the arena. Holding him in the walk by consciously keeping my energy low and my body language completely relaxed made me suddenly aware that I wasn't feeling any anxiety. This was very significant for me as I had suffered from bad anxiety every day for the last few years. So to be conscious that I didn't have anxiety in that moment was such a breakthrough. I didn't want to leave the arena, I wanted to stay in that place of calm stillness with Sunny as it was a new world to me. As I became calmer, my body completely relaxed. Sunny would have felt the tension leave my body and relaxed with me. As there was nothing in my energy or body language telling him to move fast, he slowed down so our energy levels matched.

People discover the same ability to lower their energy through many things – meditation, mindfulness, yoga, spirituality, the list goes on. You have to find out what resonates with you. Once you find it, the key is to be consistent with your practice every day. It is only with consistency that change will eventuate.

This was something I wanted to share with others. In a way, I felt it would be selfish if I didn't. I held a mini workshop for a group of my friends and they thought that what I was starting to do was amazing. So I kept developing it. I started providing lessons with Sunny, Mindy and Yogi for some young girls in the area who were struggling with bullying and self-confidence. It wasn't long before the girls were seeing changes in their lives. One of them described herself as having been 'a loud, over-the-top and constantly in-your-face kind of person'. She said that Mindy and I taught her to control her emotions and that she had calmed down so much in class and learnt to focus that her grades had gone up. Another woman said that her daughter had learnt to be assertive without being aggressive, and to watch her own child move from shy participation to confident self-expression was a true gift. Teachers and parents noticed a marked improvement in the girls' social skills, performance at school and attitude towards life. Word was quickly spreading that what I was teaching was making a difference.

It still amazes me how this program has come together. I was recently interviewed by a producer of a national current affairs show and he said to me, 'It's pretty amazing that if you had not gone through the breast cancer, which led you to move out here to the property and get your horses and ponies together, I wouldn't be sitting here interviewing you today.'

After he left, I couldn't stop thinking about what he had said. When we moved out to our property I had no thoughts of doing what I am doing today. The property and the ponies were originally just for me. But just as when I was young I had so loved introducing my friends who had been bullied to my beautiful horses to cheer them up, here I was sharing my beautiful little herd of Sunny, Mindy, Yogi and later Larry with young people who were dealing with massive challenges in their lives. I definitely feel that there is something more behind what is happening here, something I find hard to put into words. I have a strong sense that all the events of my life have led me to where I am today. Call it God, the universe, fate or serendipity, the energy and drive behind the vision seems to have a life of its own.

When I first had my idea for teaching people about horses I couldn't even think of a name for the program. I had no idea how I would advertise it. How could I possibly put into words what I was doing? It wasn't as though I had a product to sell; what I was offering was a journey of self-discovery, and how was I going to package and promote that? My brain would not rest. I would be down in the paddock picking up the horse poo when ideas and images would flash into my mind and I'd have to race up to the house and write them down so I didn't forget them. I remember sitting on the beach with two of my friends, Barbara and Tori. They specifically told me they wanted their names in this book because they helped me write my first flyer! We were at Rainbow Bay, at Coolangatta on the Gold Coast. It was a beautiful day and they were swimming and relaxing while I was huddled under an umbrella, madly scribbling away on a messy notepad. 'What are you doing?' they said. 'Why aren't you relaxing?'

I said, 'I have this idea and I don't know how to put it into words. Do you think Horses Helping Humans™ sounds good?' They said, 'That sounds great, but what the heck is it?' I tried to explain that I wanted to teach people everything I had learned, to help them deal with issues that I myself had struggled with.

My biggest challenge was articulating energy and emotion onto a flyer. I ended up with quite a few versions, some of which were quite comical when I look back on them. I was full of ideas and so passionate, but I still didn't really have the confidence to get it started. Again, it was when I was having a lesson with my Horsemanship mentor, Eliza, that I had a breakthrough. I mentioned my idea to her and she quite abruptly said, 'What are you going to call it?' I told her I'd been thinking about calling it Horses Helping Humans™. 'Well that what it's called then,' she said. 'It's Horses Helping Humans™. So when are you doing your first workshop?' After dithering for a moment, I said, 'In a month or so, I suppose.' She said, 'Pick a date right now. When are you going to do it?' I had no choice but to pick a date, and the first Horses Helping Humans™ Workshop was booked. Thank you, Eliza!

In the end I didn't need the flyers because, after my first workshop, word spread and the bookings have never stopped since, and that was nine years ago. My first workshop, which I had designed specifically for women, consisted of a small group, most of whom I knew well. I went down into the paddock and did my thing, and when it was time for us to sit down and go through the workbooks I had put together from the notes that I had jotted down having raced in from the paddock so that I wouldn't forget them, I was amazed to hear how deeply it had affected them all and how much insight it had given them into their relationships and problems. I think this was the moment I realised Horses Helping Humans™ was meant to be. Listening to them talk and seeing the looks on their faces as they described their insights was confirmation to me that what I was teaching was going to have a positive effect on people.

I then worked with small groups of young girls who lived in the local area and whose parents were concerned about them. Some had withdrawn from all family communication, some had started to self-harm, and others were acting out and not respecting any boundaries set by their parents. I still had only Sunny, Mindy and Yogi at this time, so the things I teach now about different personalities were not in place at the very start. However, I remember one day trying to get two girls to understand how they were different from each other and why they were both having problems getting their ponies to listen to them. I turned to the one with very high energy and

I said, 'You're like a can of fizzy soft drink that's been shaken up. You're way too fizzy on the inside.' I turned to the other really quiet girl and I said, 'You've got no fizz at all, that's why your horses aren't listening to you.' The fizzy girl's ask was coming across too strongly because she had so much energy and she was making Mindy very anxious. The other girl was coming across as too soft, so Sunny couldn't hear her at all.

So began my way of describing different personalities and how they come across differently in communication. I had never read any books on personality profiling nor done any quizzes myself. In fact, I wasn't even aware that there were books and quizzes on what type of personality you were. It was so simple for me to say, 'Are you like Sunny? He can get cranky real quick.' Or 'Are you like Mindy, who doesn't like arguments and can't say no?' Or 'Are you like Yogi and can't keep your mouth shut and stay focused?' The students learnt quickly the ways they were different from one another, which also helped them understand themselves.

Having been in the fitness industry for so many years and been surrounded by women who struggled with low self-esteem and poor body image, I wanted to create a program that helped women regain their self-confidence, self-respect and self-worth. Sunny and I presented my first women's workshop at a local café nestled in the rainforest of Currumbin Valley. I created a makeshift arena with tape under a big old fig tree for Sunny. When I got to the boundaries component of the workshop I said to the women, 'Leave your workbooks for now, I need you all to come outside with me.' As we walked towards the little arena, the women asked, 'Why is there a horse here?' and I said, 'Before we talk about boundaries and how to say no, I want to show you something.'

I stood in front of Sunny and adjusted my body language so it became softly extroverted, and he backed away from me immediately. I then turned and faced the women, holding the same body language and said, 'This is what "no" should look like.' No is not just a word. It is a projection of your body language so that disrespectful people don't talk you into saying yes. Disrespectful people can read introverted body language and see that you are not confident in what you are saying and know without a doubt that they can talk you into seeing things their way. At this point, some women just started to cry. It was amazing. They said, 'We've been told by so many people that we need to learn to say no, but we didn't know what it looked like.'

There was a woman attending that day from one of the big youth organisations. She thought my program would be extremely beneficial for young people, and within two weeks she had organised for the youth support co-ordinators who worked with disengaged young people from various high schools around Brisbane and the Gold Coast to attend a workshop to demonstrate to them what my program entailed. This was held at our property and I included Mindy and Yogi with Sunny, to start teaching differences in personalities. The funny thing was, even with all of those professionals attending, I didn't feel any pressure or nerves, as there was no doubt in my mind that what I was doing had value. My words and explanations flowed easily and I felt completely confident and at home in myself.

The workshop was a phenomenal success. All the youth workers felt that the visual and practical techniques I was teaching would impact positively on the young people they were working with. After that first introduction we were booked for months in advance with groups of students from all sorts of different youth organisations. Word began to spread about the results the program was getting, including fewer school suspensions, better re-engagement with school, stronger emotional control, improved confidence and an increased ability to concentrate.

We focused primarily on young people between the ages of twelve and eighteen who were at risk of early disengagement from school. Many of these students were experiencing issues that ranged from homelessness to drug and alcohol addictions, serious family trauma including domestic violence, chronic parental illness and ongoing abuse issues, anxiety and depression. Most of these students were resistant to traditional interventions, but the program resonated with them at a different level.

CHAPTER 11

Demand for the program was growing at a remarkable rate, with referrals coming from many organisations and agencies. These organisations didn't have a huge amount of money in their budget, so I had to keep the prices at an absolute minimum so that students could attend. I was working part time in the fitness industry to help support the program, and we had re-financed our house twice to keep things going.

At this time, our kitchen was being renovated and the man who came to quote saw what I was doing and mentioned that he used to be involved in running charities. 'You need to be incorporated,' he told me. 'You need to become a not-for-profit organisation so that you can be eligible for funding and tax-deductible donations.'

This was the first I had heard that I could be eligible for some financial support. However, when I received the paperwork required to become a not-for-profit organisation I was totally bamboozled. There was so much involved and, for someone like me, it was overwhelming. I put it to one side and immersed myself in my work.

During this time, I was contacted by Glenys, who had come across my business card by chance in the local chiropractor's clinic and wanted to book a session for herself and a team building session for her work colleagues. We had a marvellous session and Glenys absolutely loved the work I was doing. When I mentioned I was in the process of becoming a not-for-profit organisation and was having trouble putting together the paperwork, she offered to take it away and complete it. She returned a week later with everything filled in and little stickers indicating where I needed to sign! I couldn't believe it. It had been sitting for so long on my kitchen bench because I couldn't face deciphering it, and Glenys had sorted it out for me in a week. Since that day she has been involved in all aspects of the administration and legal side of our organisation. She is the most beautiful, gentle soul, with a heart of gold, and she has managed to bring calm order to my previously chaotic administration. Glenys is now secretary of the charity.

Finances, of course, were still very tight. Applying for any kind of funding is always difficult as there are so many organisations that need money and there is never enough to go around. Craig and I were beginning to think we might need to re-finance a third time, which was a huge concern. The program was producing such positive changes in the students that there was no way I could have walked away from it, but financially it was a terrible strain.

I then met a couple from Melbourne who, like Glenys, came for a session with me. Again, they absolutely loved what I was doing and were touched that I had developed a program for disadvantaged young people. They were particularly struck by the program's ability to reach youngsters with mental health issues. I received a phone call from them about a week after their session and they informed me that they had a foundation that supported charities for three years at a time. They had selected to support the Horse Whispering Youth Program for a three-year period. If it wasn't for this amazing couple, I honestly don't think we would have been able to continue. They also initiated the legal process for us to achieve full gift-recipient charity status, which meant that all donations to our organisation would be tax deductible.

To keep up with the number of students coming to the program, we had a grandstand erected. Thankfully we received some funding for this, which was a great relief. We extended the arena, which was a massive job because of all the earth-works that needed to be done. Our small acreage is quite hilly, so the area we use for the lessons needed to be levelled and then truckloads of fill brought in. They had to dump the fill near the house, which was the only flat area at the time, and then a bobcat made many, many trips down to the work site to level it. Oh, the dust that came through the house at that time! The day our outdoor toilet was delivered was like Christmas to me, as up until that point everyone had tramped through the house to use the house toilet. On rainy, muddy days it was a disaster zone, and on top of that, students would come out with photos from my dining room buffet wanting to know all the details of the people in the pictures and I would have to say, 'Go and put the photos back where you found them and come straight back outside so that we can get on with the lesson!'

We had all the facilities upgraded and ready to go for the influx of students, when government cuts to funding caused many organisations to close down or to have very reduced capacity. A couple of youth organisations that sent students to us daily or sent bus-loads to our workshops were closed down altogether. The youth workers were made redundant and the young people who depended on them were left without their support. It was heart-breaking. These organisations were getting disengaged young people back into study, back into school or into traineeships. I was astounded that the government would take away funding from organisations that had rock-solid results in improving youth mental health and giving them a future.

There was a particular training organisation that had a hospitality school, a hairdressing training area and also an IT room; students were known to be waiting outside to be let in on their training days and these were students who would previously never attend school or any sort of training. Young people were coming out of the organisation with the skills to gain entry into the workforce, and the fact it was shut down made me incredibly sad and angry. As well as the disappointment of the students not being able to participate in our program, I was shattered to see the effect the funding cuts had on the youth workers that I had built up such a rapport and relationship with over the last few years. The number of youth workers who became unemployed was a tragedy in itself. And last but not least was the effect the cuts had on small charities like ours that relied on the funding provided to those organisations to keep our programs open. We still had so many referrals coming through but no one had the money to pay for the students to attend. Nothing changed until February 2015 when Annastacia Palaszczuk became the Queensland premier; currently the State Government is working to restore frontline services such as youth organisations. This is a slow process, as so many services were cut. The de-funding of the peak body for youth affairs, Youth Affairs Network Queensland, was a huge loss. The previous services had been successfully established for many years, changing the lives of young people and their families. It will take a lot of work to reinstate them and employ the right staff.

I couldn't turn any students away, so we were running the program on a shoestring. Some of the parents didn't have the petrol money to drive their children out to us, so often we would pay for the students to travel out to us. There were times when I picked up the students myself. I remember one day I offered to pick up a teenage girl; she said, 'No f***ing way are you going to come and pick me up,' as she honestly did not believe I would. I told her, 'When I say I'm going to do something, I'm going to do it.' The day I was there to pick her up, she burst into tears because she didn't believe that someone would follow through on a promise.

The funding cuts continued throughout 2014. Again we were at a make-or-break stage. I was getting phone calls from an alternative educational organisation just out of Brisbane that dealt with high-risk students. I desperately wanted to put the group through the program but there were absolutely no funds to do it. Again, fate, God, the universe – whatever you want to call it – stepped in. I had done another session with a couple who were passionate about the work I was doing and they donated enough money for the students to come through the program weekly for three consecutive school terms. The changes in those particular students were extraordinary.

One young man had been sent to this specific organisation because no one else would take him on. He had a history of childhood trauma, was living in extremely difficult circum-stances and had been involved in some serious juvenile justice offences. The organisation had struggled with him for nearly a year, having great difficulty engaging with him until he realised that they were not going to give up on him. The youth workers who brought him to us said his first day with the horses was the turning point. From that day on, the young man progressed in leaps and bounds. For the first time in his life he was allowed on an overnight school camp and he was justifiably proud of achieving this as it meant he had learnt to modify his behaviour. He then continued to excel in his behaviour and learning, despite the fact that before this organisation took him on, he had been given special dispensation to leave school early. Another couple of young students made some disclosures to their case workers while they were in the calm, trusting environment of our horse program and as a result the appropriate support networks were accessed. Similarly, a couple of very aggressive students who engaged in harmful behaviours started to seek out assistance rather than act out their distress.

The helpful couple donated again after this, allowing some more groups of students to come through the program. I am full of thanks and gratitude for the generosity of all the people who have helped the Horse Whispering Youth Program continue.

CHAPTER 12

We were a couple of years into the program and I thought our little horsey family of Sunny, Yogi and Mindy was complete. My four-legged staff members! But there was one more special little guy yet to join us. The success of the program up until then had been in being able to teach the kids to understand themselves. I would say, 'Are you like Sunny? He can get cranky real quick. Or are you more like Yogi, who can't keep his mouth shut and finds it hard to focus?' While I was saying this to them, Yogi would be trying to undo people's shoelaces, pull pockets off their pants or remove their hats.

A friend of mine, Debbie, who is now an invaluable member of our charity's committee, had purchased a little buckskin pony called Koda from a lady who lived near an abattoir and had saved many horses from being slaughtered. When the miniature ponies arrived (sadly, miniatures ponies are regularly sent to the abattoir), she would always ask the manager of the abattoir if she could try to find a home for them. As she already had too many rescue horses herself, she had no room for any more. A few days after Debbie had agreed to take Koda, another little pony came in that needed to be rescued urgently and there was only a short period of time in which to do this. The man at the abattoir had said, 'Either bring me two dollars per kilo for the pony or bring him back.' When I saw the face of the little pony that urgently needed a home on a rescue website, I didn't think twice. He was a tiny grey and he reminded me a lot of Riley. He had the same little upturned nose and the same gentle look in his eye. I thought I would rescue him and then find a really good home for him. As if I'd ever have been able to give him away! I named him Larry as I figured he was 'happy as Larry' that I'd saved his life.

When I first saw Larry he was standing on his own, under a tree. He looked scared and insecure, and when I went over to him he just ran away. It took me a fair amount of time to be able to approach him. We kept Larry and Koda together at Debbie's property for the first week so that it wouldn't be too traumatic for Larry. He was a more sensitive personality than cheeky Koda, who had a personality like Yogi's. When I finally brought him home I couldn't put him in the paddock with the others as he was so traumatised and he would never have been able to stand up for himself when Yogi wanted to play. When Yogi wants to play, he's pretty full on. Larry would have got bullied. I was also worried about whether Sunny would accept Larry, as he was very protective of his little herd.

We kept Larry in our front garden for the first few weeks. It took me two weeks to gain his trust. I would bring out his dinner to feed him and he would dash to the corner of the garden and stick his nose into some bushes, with his little bottom poking out. I could imagine he was thinking, *Please don't let the human see me.* Any quick movements, picking up a rope or any sort of stick, would cause him to shake, which suggested to me that he might have been hit at some stage.

The most important thing was that Larry never feel any pressure. When you get horses from an abattoir you never know their history. The trauma of being sent away from what had once been his home, to the abattoir in a truck with horses and cattle, then taken to the lovely rescuing lady's home and finally being transported here would have been absolutely overwhelming for such a sensitive little fellow. So I took all the pressure off. I put the feed down in the middle of the garden, didn't even look at him, and walked away. I never tried to make him accept me or do anything. I just let him be. After about a week when I went out to feed him, it was his nose pointing out at me from the corner, not his fat little bottom. I was so happy, the first thing I wanted to do was rush over and pat him and say, 'Good boy!' But of course I couldn't do that because it would have put pressure on him and put him straight back in the corner. I calmly breathed out, placed his food on the ground, didn't even look at him and walked away. After a couple of days of that, he was coming closer and closer every time I put his feed down.

One particular day he was about halfway to where I fed him, so I gently placed his food on the ground, knelt down next to it with my back to him and breathed out completely. Breathing out completely around nervous ponies and horses (and, as I have learnt, around children who have experienced trauma) is imperative as it makes your energy soft and safe. When people shout or hit, they're holding their breath. When people let all of the air out of their lungs, it's very much like the air escaping a balloon or tyre – there is nothing that feels hard or intimidating about it. As I knelt there, gently breathing out, I felt Larry creeping up closer and closer to me until he was standing right at my shoulder. Larry is so little that when I was sitting on the ground his head hung naturally at shoulder height to me. I gently turned my head as I breathed out even more, and he pushed his forehead up against mine. Tears started to well up in my eyes as he was telling me that he trusted me. Again my first instinct was to put my hand up, give him and rub and say, 'Good boy,' but our relationship was still at a very fragile stage. Any movement from me at that time would have sent him straight back into his corner, so I had to breathe out even more, turn my head away from him and quietly and gently walk away. It was that moment of taking all pressure off Larry that built the trust between us, as he realised I would never take advantage of him.

Within a few days he was following me all around the garden. Mindy was quite put out as she could see that Larry had become the new porch pony. There was one particular day when I was lying down on a deckchair reading a book and Larry came along and lifted the book out of my hands with his mouth and then rested his nose on my tummy. It was absolutely beautiful. Hidden under this shy, nervous pony was quite a cheeky sense of humour, and we see it in him now when he stirs up the others at playtime and then quickly runs to safety so that he doesn't get involved in their rough play.

We have a cattle dog, Karma, who is cheeky too and I was constantly complaining about her throwing the cushions from my outdoor couch all over the lawn. She was always getting the blame. One morning I looked out the window and there was Larry with one of my good couch cushions swaying from his mouth as he took it across the lawn, dropped it and then went back for another one. I opened the door, he turned to look at me with a cushion in his mouth (his expression was priceless) and I said to him, 'So you are actually a really cheeky little boy.' I was so happy, as his personality was starting to flourish because I hadn't put any pressure on him and had allowed him to be himself. I do the same thing with the young people who come here. There is never any expectation at any time and there's always complete acceptance so that personalities can flourish and grow with confidence.

As I could see that Larry's confidence was growing every day and Sunny, Mindy and Yogi were being very sociable with him over the fence, I felt it was now time to take Larry out of the front yard so that he could join the rest of our four-legged family in the paddock. I was so happy to see that when Yogi ran over and started to become quite boisterous with Larry, Larry turned his bottom towards Yogi and, with a very loud squeal, lashed his legs out three or four times. This was fabulous, as Yogi can get very dominant with other ponies and this was Larry's way of saying, 'I will play rough to a certain level but then that is as far as it will go.' Sunny accepted Larry beautifully, and funnily enough it was Mindy who was very reserved around their new companion. It has taken a couple of years for Mindy to completely accept Larry and only now will she allow him to share some of her food, and only when she's in the right mood. Some days she will happily let him share her hay and then on other days, with ears flat back and a high-pitched squeal, she tells him to get away. He stands there looking so confused, as if to say, 'But it was okay yesterday.' I say to Larry at these times, 'Get used to it, sweetie. She can be a bit moody.'

Because of what happened to Riley, I was very conscious that Larry never be put in a dangerous situation. So I partitioned the corners of the paddock with some tape at about waist height, so if he ever felt the pressure was too much at playtime, he could run into his little safe zone. As it was so low, he could duck under it and none of the others could get to him. He used this regularly and still does, but the difference is that now he will turn his little fat bottom towards Yogi and send out a few short, swift kicks before he runs away. Watching him initiate play always brings a smile to my face. His tail will go right up, he'll prance around looking like a little Arab nipping Yogi on the bottom, speeding very quickly past Sunny until everyone is racing around, and then he'll dash back to his safe corner when the going gets too rough. When they all stop playing, he'll come out prancing around again with a look on his face as if to say, 'Why have you stopped?'

Larry has become such a valuable part of our program here. He has represented everything I stand for. He's been through a really rough time and he's had to learn to trust again. He's had to learn that was then and this is now and he can have a good life when he puts the past behind him.

One of the things that we do with our horses is rub them all over with our direction sticks. In Natural Horsemanship terms, they are 'carrot sticks'. These may look like whips; however, they are not! Whips are not used in Natural Horsemanship as we never hit horses. We simply use the sticks to give direction and create energy. For example, if we are asking our horses to circle around us, we point our arm and leg in the direction we want them to go and then, with the other hand, lift the stick out towards the other side of our body and give it a flick to create some energy. We always start our sessions by rubbing the horses all over with our direction sticks so they know that any time the stick is lifted during these session, it's never to hurt them.

The first time we attempted to rub Larry with a stick, he was horrified. His little eyes were rolling; he could not keep his legs still. So again I used the advance-retreat method: each time I put the stick on his back to rub him I calmly left it there until he stood still and then I gently took it away. We did this a few times until he learnt that when the stick was rested on his back it actually meant relaxing time! When it got to the stage where he would finally stand still and let us rub him all over with the stick, it was such an achievement for him.

I didn't want to put Larry under any pressure so when I started using him in our workshops, he wasn't given too many tasks. All the students who come here complete a horse agility course. They circle their horses or ponies around them; they ask them to go from trot to walk with their breathing; they back them through L-shapes, lead them with no ropes around markers and get them to jump over little obstacles. One day a young student was standing with Larry by one of the jumps. Larry watched all the others go through the course, then he looked at the jump, then at me, then back at the jump. Next thing, his tiny legs took off and he flew over the jump like a showjumper. He then stopped and turned around and looked at me and I said, 'Oh my gosh, I've just found your talent.' Now, Larry absolutely loves to jump our little course.

On show day, he's always the star when it comes to jumping. Yogi will just walk straight through the jump, or when he's asked to trot over a jump, he'll stop and then climb up onto the jump stand and proceed to paw the air, demanding a scratch halfway through the show. Sunny always makes a half-hearted attempt at lurching over the jump in a very ungainly manner, as he certainly does not have the grace of a showjumper! Mindy thinks she's a princess and shouldn't have to jump at all, but Larry flies over the jump, tail in the air, legs tucked up under his belly, and clears it by a mile. Everyone cheers and he looks so happy with himself.

CHAPTER 13

As the reputation of our program grew, universities and colleges began showing an interest in sending their third-year psychology students to do their placement hours or their 50-hour community internship with us. I greatly appreciated it as they contributed so much to our program. One of the lecturers, Rhonda Purton, from the Australian College of Applied Psychology in Brisbane came to assess my program to see if it was suitable for their students to do some of their placement hours with me. Since Larry had arrived I had been giving students the choice of four horsey personalities to pick from. I felt that if they could relate to one of the personalities, they would be able to understand themselves better and see how they came across to others.

Rhonda spent quite a few sessions here and said to me at the end of her assessment that she was absolutely amazed at the framework I had put in place. I told her I had no framework; I hadn't planned any of it, I was just using what I had. She then went on to tell me that my theoretical underpinnings were perfectly aligned with the four temperaments they taught at the college.

Apparently the explanation I was giving for Sunny was spot on for what they termed the choleric temperament: quick decision makers, like to lead, strong personality, very protective of those close to them, and may come across as intimidating to more introverted types. Mindy matches the explanation I give for the melancholy temperament: more introverted, sensitive, finds it hard to say no, cautious and quite intimidated by aggressive personalities. Yogi represents an absolute sanguine: extroverted, fun-loving, compulsive, gets bored very easily, can find it hard to focus and will talk easily and often.

Now this is where it really gets amazing. Larry was our missing fourth temperament: the easygoing, phlegmatic type, easy to get along with, a good mediator, a more quiet sense of humour and a great organiser.

This was why Rhonda thought I had a framework and had specifically gone out and searched for ponies with these traits. Of course this was not the case at all, it had all just happened naturally, and as Larry had come along as a rescue pony, I had no idea of the kind of pony he was – if he'd been another

Yogi personality the program wouldn't have been as success-ful. We needed an example of all four temperaments, so that everyone who came to us could relate to one of them.

Rhonda was absolutely amazed that everything had fallen into place in such a structured way and without me planning it. She said that she had come out in goose bumps! I said, 'Now that you've told me all that, I've come out in goose bumps too, because I had no idea. I've never even heard of the four temperaments!'

While the personality profile for each horse was useful for learning, I was in no way humanising the horses. My years of professional experience with horses meant that I made sure I emphasised safety as horses do not think, nor act, like humans. However, they all have distinct personalities of their own. If I am doing anything, I am 'horse-anising' humans! I am simply giving people an easy-to-understand guide to the differences in people's temperaments.

After working with these four temperaments for many years now, I have seen just how accurate they are. Disadvantaged youngsters as well as corporate CEOs easily identify with these traits when they are taught them with a sense of humour. It's important that we don't take ourselves too seriously or become judgemental about the way we are or about the way other people are. We need to appreciate the positive attributes of everybody's temperament, as well as what other temperaments have to offer us in our lives.

When I meet trembling melancholy Mindys (some have been abused and bullied very badly), I see myself when I was bullied and disrespected by people who never took no for an answer. I can feel their fear and anxiety. When I meet sanguine Yogis, I see myself back in school when I felt stupid and worthless as I didn't know how to focus and thought no one would ever understand me. I can feel their lack of self-confidence and sense that their acting-out behaviour is simply to cover how they are actually feeling. The choleric Sunny personalities struggle with aggression, and I can feel their frustration at having to put on a front all the time as they feel that if they soften in any way they will appear weak. Phlegmatic Larrys try so hard to keep the peace, and I know how much anxiety that causes as people-pleasing is exhausting and gave me years of stress.

I see and feel these emotions as if they were my own. This gift of picking up on other people's feelings used to be detrimental to my health as I didn't understand it. I would feel taken over by other people's emotions and energy. I thought that everybody felt this, as it was so normal to me. When I started this program I realised what a gift this was. Being able to pick up on the slightest change in body language allows me to sense the true story behind the words being spoken, and to be able to make people aware of this themselves in their communications is a privilege. Now I know what my hyper-sensitivity is for. It is like an antenna that I use to relate to people and to connect with those who don't feel like they deserve connection.

The four distinct temperaments are so important to the program as they don't only make people aware of what traits they have, but also how they come across to temperaments different from their own. When my choleric students identify themselves, they get excited because they think they're going to work with the big strong Sunny horse. I tell them, 'No, you're not working with Sunny. You're going to come over here and meet Larry.' And they go, 'That little pony? I thought I'd be working with the big horse!' What they learn with Larry immediately is that their strong choleric energy completely freaks him out. His legs start to move really fast as he's trying to get away from them, and his beautiful big eyes roll. The choleric students always say, 'What's wrong with the pony?' I tell them that their energy is very strong and it's making Larry feel really uncomfortable. I teach them how to breathe out completely and relax their body and it isn't too long before Larry will quietly come towards them and lean against their leg. As by this stage they are aware of the importance of keeping their energy down, they usually say in a whisper, 'What's he doing now?' And I very quietly say back to them, 'Because you've completely relaxed and breathed out, you're making him feel safe.'

Sometimes this can be the start of a change in students who have struggled with aggression. For the first time they feel what it's like to have something feel safe with them instead of being scared of them. They start to see strength in softness. When they have contact with Larry on a weekly basis, consciously keeping themselves calm and relaxed, they form such a beautiful bond with our little pony. It often brings tears to our eyes when we see these previously aggressive young people softly and gently asking Larry to pop over jumps and complete the obstacle course on show day.

When the melancholy temperaments – my very shy, introverted students – say, 'Yes, I'm a Mindy,' they think they are going to work with the beautiful, gentle soft pony. I then give them the news that they're going to work with the big strong Sunny horse! They always have an expression of 'Oh no!' on their face, but when they come over to meet Sunny and he gently breathes on them and nuzzles them, their fear starts to dissipate. What they learn with Sunny is that if they ask him to do any of the tasks when their body language is introverted and they don't look confident, he ignores them. They always say to me, 'Sunny's not listening to me!' And I reply, 'It's not that he's not listening it's that he can't hear you because your body language doesn't match what you're asking for.'

Mindys need to learn that the more they show respect for themselves by having confident body language, the more respect Sunny types, horses and people, will have for them.

When people lose confidence, especially through being bullied, their body language becomes introverted: their shoulders are slumped and forward of their hips, their arms are very close to their body and their mid-section is closed off. Self-respect lives under your rib cage so it's important that Mindys open up their body language so they are heard. I teach them to stand like a puffer fish! A puffer fish has always got its fins away from its body and looks like it's taking up space. I then get them to imagine they're wearing a big shiny belt buckle and when they're speaking to people they want to show it off. Showing off your big shiny belt buckle teaches introverts to keep their hips in front of their shoulders so that they don't look like they're feeling intimidated. It allows self-respect to project from them, and other people unconsciously pick up on this.

It's amazing to see the look on the faces of Mindy students when they go from trying to ask Sunny to back away from them with their normal introverted body language to standing like a puffer fish and showing Sunny their shiny belt buckle and to see him immediately back away from them and show respect for their personal space. Sometimes this will be the first time an introverted Mindy has felt what it's like to be in control of their body language and self-respect. It's a very empowering moment for them. And on show day it's profoundly moving to see students who have previously been abused or bullied confidently putting big strong Sunny through all the obstacles, looking calm and confident the whole time.

The phlegmatic students, the Larrys of this world, work with Mindy or Sunny. Mindy seems to think she's a bit of a princess and doesn't need to do any work apart from having her beautiful mane brushed by the students. When Mindy is asked to approach any of the obstacles, the face she pulls is so funny, as she actually looks disgusted and mortified. It's so easy for phlegmatic Larrys to get caught up in trying to do things too perfectly; their shoulders will tighten up without realising it and they'll start looking defensive. This is a classic phlegmatic body language when under pressure; it's not an aggressive defensiveness, it's a self-protection mechanism. They want to make sure they are respected and heard but the tight shoulders will send a different message. Larrys have a quiet (sometimes cheeky) sense of humour, and drawing on their natural lightness instead of their perfectionism opens more doors of communication. Tight shoulders with Mindy can make her more stubborn because, to her, they are telling her what to do, they are not asking her, so Larrys have to stay very relaxed through their shoulders and confident so that Mindy will respect them.

Both phlegmatic and melancholy personalities often just go, 'Oh it's all right, Mindy. You don't have to do anything. We'll just take you over to the fence and give you a cuddle.' But these students need to learn how to say no to people who try to manipulate them into doing what they want. Mindy's usually quite apprehensive of new students, but once she trusts them she gets quite bossy. She likes to decide when it's time to stop, or when it's time to leave the arena and go to her stable. It's quite common to see Mindy leading students to where she would like to go. She may be short but she's incredibly wide and round, with about a two hundred kilo towing ability to take students wherever she decides! The students have to learn to be calmly assertive with her, then her respect for them slowly grows. It's empowering when these students realise that they can get Mindy to do the things they ask by being softly assertive.

Yogi's part in the program is such an eye-opener for my young sanguine temperaments who find it hard to focus or have ADD or ADHD. I match them with Yogi and I let them know before they even start working with him that he's going to show them just how frustrating they can be when it looks like they're not paying attention. Usually as soon as the students start working with him, they turn to me and say, 'He's not even listening. He's just doing his own thing. It's like we're not even here.' I turn to them and say with a laugh, 'It's annoying, isn't it?' They get it and understand straight away how they come across at times. The focusing techniques I teach them are the very same focusing techniques they need to use when interacting with humans. I show them how they can look like they're really interested in everything that is being said to them and then, without them realising it, by prac-tising these skills they actually do begin to hear what is being said to them.

Sanguine Yogi personalities have a habit of either fidgeting or moving their eyes around when people are talking to them. This makes it seem as though they aren't listening and are being disrespectful. I know from my own personal experience how hard it is for a Yogi to stay focused through any situation, so I teach them that they need to stand still and imagine they have laser beams coming out of their eyes towards the person speaking to them. This changes the way Yogis come across to other people altogether. All of a sudden they look calm and focused, which is respectful. Yogis are often amazed at how much they actually start to take in and learn once they use the keeping-still-and-laser-beaming technique.

For people of all ages to accept the temperament they've been born with is very important as, in my view, Sunny Cholerics have such a strong natural leadership personality because they are meant to make people feel safe. Yogi Sanguines' energy is there to motivate people. Mindy Melancholys, who are very sensitive, make people feel cared for, and Larry Phlegmatics help make people feel secure. This is why it's so important that we accept the differences in one another and appreciate what each temperament can bring into our lives.

By now the Department of Child Services was utilising our program regularly. We were working with students and families who had a whole range of challenges: drug and alcohol addictions, mental health issues, domestic violence within their families, and some who had committed criminal offences. Bringing families to attend together helps them immensely in their ongoing counselling sessions. Sometimes they have been through dreadful trauma or domestic violence, or a mother may have been released from jail and her children come out of foster care to be returned to her. As families may have been apart for a while, or may struggle communicating with one another, it's important they form some understanding of each other and are given some positive communication skills.

It's lovely to see the change in families through our program. When they arrive they can be quite detached from one another, even uncomfortable together. By the end of the workshop they are smiling and laughing about being a Mindy, a Yogi, a Larry or a Sunny and have learnt a different way to speak to one another with calmness and respect.

It's my belief that from a young age we should all learn to understand who we are, how we come across to others and how we can communicate effectively through awareness of our body language. I have seen significant changes in students once they learn these skills, and this affects everyone around them in a positive way. Because of this I developed a PowerPoint program called Which Horse or Pony Are You?, which can be taught in schools. It has become very popular, with Sunny, Yogi, Mindy and Larry in cartoon form demonstrating the specific body language each temperament displays (these cartoons have also become very popular in my corporate presentations). Also using live footage of them helps me to explore our four different horsey temperaments. I also discuss anxiety and depression and what they feel like. I encourage students to not feel embarrassed by their emotions and to speak to their school counsellor if they are feeling upset. This helps younger students recognise the differences between themselves and their classmates, as well as their family members so they can all get along better. This also helps the teachers better identify the body language of different personalities so they can interact with the students on an individual level.

CHAPTER 14

People are often surprised to learn that they can communicate with a horse by learning what different body language displays mean. A horse's ear positions (back, forward, one to the side or back, flat back), eyes (wide, squinty or other), tight or loose lips, the carriage of their neck and the tightness or relaxation throughout their bodies – each says a different thing about a horse.

When the alpha horse wants his dinner and there are other horses in the way, he will pin his ears back flat and charge through the middle of the herd to get to his food. If a pony feels threatened, he will swing his body around so that his bottom is facing whatever is intimidating him, pin his ears right back, raise his head, lift his tail and squeal very loudly, which says, 'Back off!' When the alpha horse wants another horse to turn around and face him (as it's respectful to show your head not your bottom), he will direct all his attention and energy on that more submissive horse's rear end, until that horse swings around and gives his full attention. When two horses are nose to nose, sorting out issues, it is always the more dominant horse that walks forward and causes the other horse to walk backward.

When it's time to play, heads are tossed, tails are flicked and there is a big surge of adrenaline as everyone starts to gallop around. To more timid horses, play can be a bit scary as it can get rough. Larry always uses his safety area at play time. He will often cause the play – he will start prancing with his tail in the air, nip Yogi a few times on the bottom – but once everyone's energy is up high, he makes a quick exit to keep himself safe.

The lessons I teach in my horsemanship classes helps enormously in the development of communications in everyday life. Just like there are many people who don't understand when their horse is becoming uncomfortable, there are also many people who don't recognise when the people they are speaking to are getting uncomfortable.

I teach people to be conscious of the body language and energy they need to use in human to human communication. My students develop the ability to diffuse situations that are starting to get reactive, to spot when someone is starting to disengage from a conversation and help get them back on track, to learn when to speak and know when not to speak, how to ask, not tell, and to be conscious of staying respectful at all times. It's so rewarding to give students, who struggle so much with focus, techniques to help them understand what I'm teaching. They are often amazed by how much they have learned. I just tell them, you've always had the ability to learn, you just didn't know how to tune in to the learning channel (another Sue-ism!).

I use very basic horsemanship ground skills to show students, not just how their body language and energy effects their horse, but also how their body language and energy effects the people around them. Each personality type will have different body language adjustments to make and whatever they adjust in these exercises, is what they'll need to adjust when communicating with humans. The simple act of asking your horse or pony to back out of your personal space can tell a lot. Some students ask too hard, some too soft, some do not have confident body language.

Ground skills can very quickly give students a sense of achievement as they are building confidence in themselves as well as in their horse or pony. It is the simplicity of my program that makes it so popular. Also, a positive outcome is very encouraging when learning something new. Humans must remain calm and assertive to master these basic ground skills and it is through this that students develop self-respect.

Every time Sunny or one of the ponies stops, looks at their human and states quite clearly, 'I don't want to do that,' the student has to calmly repeat the correct signals, 'That's what I would like you to do,' without getting emotional, and then they have to negotiate calmly and assertively until the task is completed. It is always a turning point in the students' emotional development. They learn very quickly that becoming emotional (frustrated, anxious) puts their horse or pony into a reactive state. As soon as they calm themselves down and relax, they can see that their horse or pony also becomes relaxed. This gives them a very clear indication of how they come across to other people when they are becoming overemotional. It's the calm assertiveness that builds the respect.

The next ground-skill exercise I teach is how to lead your horse correctly. Sometimes you will see people getting dragged along by their horse, other times you will see humans pulling their horses along. Neither looks remotely like any sort of partnership. This is where I'm teaching my students how to use their energy and their body language to suggest that their horse or pony walks forward. It's funny, but Mindy will not lead if she's told to lead. If someone barges in front of her and pulls the lead rope for her to follow them, she will not move. They often say, 'Why won't she come with me?' I say, 'Well would you like to be dragged along at the end of a rope? How about you go back and stand next to her, point your body the way you would like to go, lift your energy, give her a gentle pat in the middle of her back and ask her to walk with you.' As soon as the student asks politely and respectfully, Mindy is happy to walk with them.

When Larry is led, students must remain very calm. I can always tell when they are using respectful energy, as Larry's head drops down very low and he walks, relaxed, alongside them. If his head pops up and his ears go back I know I have a little more work to do with that student's energy.

Yogi is like the larrikin you get in the classroom or work-place. He feeds off laughter and being the centre of attention. When the students laugh because they can't get him to move, it actually makes Yogi more disrespectful. Learning to be very still and very direct with human Yogi sanguines is quite a skill. They pick up that when you are still and then you ask, you actually mean business. When you fidget and laugh when trying to communicate with a Yogi personality, you're actually giving them permission to fidget and laugh and it takes away the importance of what you are trying to say to them.

The next exercise I give my students is circling their ponies or horse on a twelve-foot lead rope. Mindy Melancholys who are working with Sunny must make their body language very open and clear when they point the way they want him to go. Sunny often races off in the opposite direction as, being a strong leadership personality, he believes he knows the best way to do everything. This can be daunting to an introverted Mindy. They have to actually shake the rope as they turn with him until he stops, turns around and looks at them. I say to them, 'What you're doing here is saying, "Excuse me. I didn't want you to go that way. You must wait until I'm ready to send you, as that's safe and respectful."' Often Sunny will race off again in the direction he would like to go and the student has to repeat the request, in no way backing down but holding their calm, assertive decision for him to go the way they are directing him, looking very strong but staying very soft and polite with their body language.

When Larry is circling he tends to race off before he is asked. As he is a different personality from Sunny, Larry racing off to complete the circle means something entirely different to Sunny's attitude of wanting to take over. Larry's reason for taking off very quickly is because he thinks he'll get in trouble if he doesn't do the job. A lot of the students go, 'Oh isn't it great, he's running around on his own.' I say, 'No, it's not great. He's actually reacting to you, not responding to you.' This is one of the key points that strong Sunny personalities need to remember in the workplace and at home. It's very important for the stronger Sunny personalities to realise that when Larry is reacting to them; they're not working in partnership together. Sunny Cholerics need to completely breathe out, relax their shoulders, give their rope a little jiggle as if to say, 'Hey little dude, no need to stress, just wait until I'm ready. It's all good.' As they breathe out and relax more, Larry feels comfortable to just stand and relax. All they have to do with Larry is the slightest pointing of their finger and he will move off in a nice relaxed manner.

Again, the same exercise teaches students who are working with Mindy a different lesson. How often do we ask people to do things for us and then they make us feel so sorry for them we end up doing it ourselves? Mindy is the classic, because when students ask her to circle, her great big eyes slowly blink at them and they feel so sorry for her that they feel bad asking her to do anything. This is a good lesson for people who get manipulated easily. They understand that Mindy's respect for them increases when they ask her to complete her task, and she learns that her reward comes at the end of the session, not halfway through.

The students with Yogi usually have the biggest struggle getting him to move around in a circle because you only get out of Yogi what you put into him. Yogi humans have to learn to focus all of their energy towards Yogi while presenting an enthusiastic persona, otherwise he will think, *What's the point of doing that?* When Yogi students do work experience here or help out, I have to make sure it's really motivating. For example, 'Oh, how cool is this going to be today, we're going to paint the fence. Let's have a competition to see who gets covered in the least paint.' Yogi Sanguines always gets covered in paint, ponies and humans!

The biggest test is when we take all halters and ropes off and the students, using only their body language and energy, have to get their horse or pony to complete an agility course. Again this is a moment when Sunny sometimes takes off because he knows exactly what he needs to do. He will jump the jump by himself or continue circling, even when asked to stop. Mindy students have to really hold it together and use clear, calm, assertive energy to get their horse back. It's wonderful to see Sunny bobbing his head and licking his lips with acceptance and respect. They are now ready to complete the course because they now have Sunny's full respectful attention.

Working without the halter and the rope with Larry can be just as challenging. Because of his nervous energy, it is important to stay relaxed so that he doesn't think you're chasing him around. This is sometimes quite a challenge for a human Sunny as the more he runs around, the more impatient they get, but they soon realise the only way to settle their pony down is to settle themselves down. This is a big lesson for partners in relationships as they see quite clearly that their frustrated energy can cause quite acute anxiety in nervous types. As soon as they take all the emotional pressure off Larry, he stops, turns around and faces them, pops his little ears forward and then gently walks in and stands by their side as if to say, 'I'm ready to work with you now, as I feel safe with you, not scared.'

What Yogi does as soon as he's at liberty is amble over to the jump and stand on the jump stand. Once he's sick of that he will lie down and sometimes not get up. Other times he'll roll back and forward rubbing his hairy back into the sand, having a wonderful time. When the students are laughing, they can't get Yogi to listen to them because in a way they are encouraging him. This is when the skill of standing incredibly still and being very direct with Yogi makes him realise that you mean what you say. And even though you might be a bit of a larrikin like Yogi, there are times when you have something really important to say and you need to be heard.

Learning to identify the different temperaments you live or work with can make such a difference to your stress levels. When you understand how to communicate with others through body language and energy, or to defuse reactions and encourage responses, relationships change.

The students attending our program struggle with such a range of issues that I have literally had to learn on the run how to handle all the different situations that crop up. It has been during these situations that my 'Sue-isms' have evolved! These are sayings or strategies that I use all the time because I have found that they work.

I always try to keep a level of humour in situations and make sure people never feel like I am disrespecting them or putting them down. For example, I had a group of three teenage girls attend my program as they all had a problem with anger and aggression. On this particular day I had turned away from the arena for a moment to get a jump pole, leaving my assistant, who I had been training for over twelve months, in the paddock with the girls. In the few moments I was gone, I could hear some very loud shouting and swearing coming from the training area. I hurried straight back and I could hear one of the girls yelling, 'You're a slag.' Another shouted, 'You're a skank,' and the third one yelled, 'Well you're both sluts.' I held my hands away from my body and said, 'Hang on! What's the difference between a slag, a skank and a slut? I thought they all meant the same thing.' They all started telling me what the difference was. This meant I'd 'changed the direction of the conversation' – a very useful strategy, I've found. Instead of abusing each other, they all instantly turned around and started educating me on what the differences were, which put them back on the same team.

They were all very pleased that they had managed to teach Sue a thing or two, and things settled down very quickly. Eventually I was able to ask, 'By the way, what started all of that?' It turned out that one of the girls had turned to another while she was trying to back Mindy up and told her that she wasn't doing it right. The girl with Mindy told her to get stuffed (only in not such polite terms), and then the third one joined in and off they went. I turned that into a positive lesson on how negatively reacting to things blows them right out of proportion and that suggesting or commenting on something must not come across as telling. I also explained that we never want to call each other names and that name-calling can only make things worse. It was so lovely to see all of those girls leaving with big smiles on their faces and as best of friends, as it had become quite a bonding session. The importance of defusing a situation before you start discussing the issue that is causing the problem is paramount. The issue cannot be resolved when everyone's emotions are still high.

Another good example of when I 'changed the direction of the conversation' was when I had a group of students sitting around the table in our grandstand at lunchtime and I was asking them what they wanted to do when they returned to studying. All of the students were sharing their hopes and ambitions when one of the young boys, who enjoyed scaring people and had quite a reputation for shocking people with horror stories, turned to me and said, 'I want to work with chopped-up dead bodies.' I didn't react, I just said, 'How cool is that. You want to be a forensic scientist like the people on *CSI*. That's fantastic! You're going to be such an amazing professional person.' The look on his face was priceless. He was so used to shocking people and having them react with disgust, which he loved, but when I reacted by being proud of his career selection, it actually started him thinking. I could see him begin to realise that it felt better to impress people than to scare the living daylights out of them. So all of a sudden, working towards a career became cool.

Another young man had been arrested for stealing training equipment out of a personal trainer's van. Within a week of stealing the equipment he was teaching boxing lessons to some of the local young kids, using all the pads and gloves he'd stolen. He was making a small fortune for a thirteen-year-old! After spending time with him I learnt that he had been brought up in a family where crime was a way of life. He was as bright as a button. He absolutely loved coming to my program and I could see the potential he had. After hearing about the boxing classes I said to him, 'Do you know what an entrepreneur is?'

He replied, 'No, miss, I've never heard that word in my life.'

I proceeded to explain to him how an entrepreneur's mind works; how they see possibility and opportunity where other people may not. I googled a few young entrepreneurs to show him how these people had started life with either learning difficulties or family dysfunction, yet had gone on and forged successful careers. I sat down with him and said, 'You have the ability to go a long way in your life without ever being dishonest. You have the ability to really make something of yourself and change the pattern of the family life you have known. I'm not impressed with you taking the personal trainer's equipment, and it's really important that you understand how difficult it was for him to not be able to work for a few weeks as it was his only form of income. He may not have been able to pay his rent or buy food; he may have not been able to support his children. I want you to understand that when you take things from others it can affect many people in many different ways. That aside, I'm impressed with the way your mind works, how fast you learn and how committed you've been to the program, and the way you've always given me and the horses so much respect. Using all of these skills towards something you would like to do will mean that you can be successful without ever being at risk of going to jail. You can earn money by being honest.'

The way he looked at me broke my heart. He had tears in his eyes and he said, 'Thank you, miss, no one has ever said anything like that to me before.' So my learning point here was, 'Okay, you've done something pretty bad, but understanding the consequences of what you did to someone and how it affected them can help you to think very carefully about your actions in the future.' Some people don't care what they do to other people; others honestly don't understand how detrimental an action can be. Once they do understand the effects of their actions and are genuinely remorseful, the focus then turns to the positive abilities they have so that they can move forward with these, to help people instead of hurting them.

Another Sue-ism I use is 'Show us your shiny belt buckle!' I use it to show very shy young men how to walk as if they feel confident and this in turn makes them look confident. As I've mentioned before, when you walk with an introverted body language you can become a target for bullies. When I work with men in the corporate world, if they are Larry Phlegmatics personalities I teach them how to walk like John Wayne or Clint Eastwood. They have to imagine that they've got a big belt buckle on, and walk with a cowboy swagger, as what it does is tilt their hips in front of their shoulders, which makes them look more confident. I was working with a group of students one day and I was trying to explain to a very shy young man how to walk with a different body language. His elbows were literally locked to his side, his arms were across the front of his body, and his shoulders were hunched and tight. He was portraying indecisiveness and zero confidence. These students had not seen many cowboy movies, so I was trying to think of a more familiar example. As the young man was walking around with Sunny and I was trying to get him to walk differently, one of the more extroverted boys (a Sunny Choleric) yelled out across the arena, 'You've got to walk like the Brax brothers off *Home and Away!*' (*Home and Away* is a well-known Australian soap opera; the Brax brothers are the tough guys in the show.)

The Sunny Choleric was standing on the edge of the arena giving his advice, of course while using his Sunny body language. I stopped the session for a moment and said to my shy young man, 'Look at how Sunny Boy over there is standing. See how his arms are away from his sides?' He replied, 'Do you want me to try and look tough?' I said, 'No, no. I want you to look relaxed and confident.' There is such a fine line between looking confident and slightly aggressive. I turned to Sunny Boy and brought to his attention the way he was standing with his natural confidence, but if at any time he tightened his shoulders and held his breath, he might give the impression that he wanted to start an argument.

Immediately my shy young man understood the difference between tough and confident and he completely relaxed his shoulders, opened his chest, held his arms away from his body and started strutting around the arena with Sunny following him compliantly. It was another day that brought a smile to my face.

I tell young people walking into job interviews and corporate men walking into boardrooms to use this 'shiny belt buckle' technique, You will often hear me shouting across the paddock, 'Show your belt buckle so your horse will take notice of you!'

For young girls and women, this Sue-ism is called, 'Puff 'n' pop your piercing'. Now this one is only for Mindy Melancholys and Larrys Phlegmatics as Yogi Sanguines and Sunny Cholerics do this naturally and we don't want to give them any more body language projection as it will scare people out of the room! Puff 'n' pop your piercing means softly opening your body language by taking your arms away from your sides, keeping your shoulders very relaxed and imagining you have a beautiful piercing in your belly button that you are very proud of. When they feel nervous and intimidated by strong personalities, Larrys get very tight shoulders and can look defensive. Mindys will keep their hands across the front of their bodies and look intimidated and nervous. When they breathe out and relax, take their arms away from their body and imagine popping out their belly piercing so their self-respect pops out like a superpower, extroverted personalities are more inclined to hear their words.

So many girls have told me this helps them deal with bullies. I've had emails from women all over the country who have used my shiny belt buckle in boardrooms, courtrooms and in high-level corporate negotiations. It always puts the biggest smile on my face when I hear that they have success-fully pulled off a 'people whisper' (another Sue-ism). As I tell everyone who does my program, I'm teaching them the very basics of horse whispering so that they can transfer it straight into people whispering.

CHAPTER 15

My corporate team-building workshops began when some of the parents of our students sat in on the sessions. They told me that they were learning so much about themselves and the dynamics of their family just by listening to me describing the differences between Sunny, Mindy, Larry and Yogi, and how to communicate with them differently. Parents who were business owners started to ask me if I did corporate training and before too long management teams were being sent to me for workshops. Again, word quickly got around and corporate groups began flying in from interstate and even from overseas.

As I started working in the corporate sector, I was horrified to discover that there is as much intimidation and fear in some workplaces as there is for those young people who live on the streets. I find it appalling that some people dread going to work because of the disrespect of some of their colleagues.

I cannot stress strongly enough that when teams learn about the differences in each other's temperaments and how to communicate with one another effectively without being reactive, the dynamic of the whole team changes and that is when true productivity begins. People actually start working together, not against one another. Opinions can be given, not forced. People can be asked, not told. People can be heard without being shut down. Respect and dignity is restored.

In the corporate workshops, I delve deeper into the psychology of communication and provide a lot more information about body language. Most of the people who attend are working under a great deal of pressure every day. They need to learn how to read body language and assess situations very quickly and to drop their energy before they trigger a reaction in somebody else. When they learn the importance of having relaxed body language, while at the same time speaking calmly and respect-fully, the outcomes of those situations are greatly enhanced.

One corporate story that always puts the biggest smile on my face concerns a lovely gentleman called David. He was a dignified, respectful Larry Phlegmatic. His body language was introverted and he was very quiet. David had built his company up from scratch in Australia and had then opened an office overseas, which he was justifiably proud of. The problem was he had employed some very gung-ho, go-getting, strong Sunny Cholerics to run the overseas office. David was finding that he felt nauseous and filled with dread as he walked into his overseas boardroom as he would be talked over and not heard by the loud, extroverted, disrespectful Sunnys and Yogis. (I must mention here that not all Sunnys and Yogis are disrespectful. I myself am a Yogi/Sunny (sanguine/choleric), but like many others, I'm a respectful one. I'm talking about the personalities that are running unchecked.)

I said, 'Righto, we're going to change things around a bit. Show me how you walk into that boardroom. What are you carrying? What do you look like when they get their first glimpse of you?' He told me that when the lift doors opened he could see the boardroom; he would step out of the lift with his briefcase in one arm and his laptop tucked up under the other, then proceed to walk into the boardroom, sit at his seat and place his briefcase and his laptop neatly in front of him. He would start the meeting, but he would find that he just wasn't getting the respect he deserved and they would talk over him or at him.

We had to start right from the beginning. We had to make sure he was fully relaxed before he even entered that room. I explained that while he was travelling up to the office in the lift he needed to rock back and forth on his heels, his body completely relaxed. I call this 'releasing the confidence hormone' (there's one of my Sue-isms again) as it makes you conscious that you've got a whole body; you're not just a ball of nervous tension stuck tight in your upper body. You've dropped your energy down, you're relaxed and you've grounded yourself so that your whole body is present when you walk into the room.

At the same time he needed to follow a breathing technique that I call 'jelly belly breathing'. One of the exercises I teach people is how to bring their horses from trot to walk on the end of a twelve-foot rope simply by breathing out. When you breathe out and completely relax your belly, it turns your energy down and your horse can feel that. So when you're thinking *walk* and your whole body is saying 'walk', your horse will feel the change in your energy. That is how our horses here relate to what is being asked of them in the sessions. If you don't completely relax your stomach when you're doing deep breathing your stress hormone will still be pumping. When you get nervous and anxious, or even frustrated, your subconscious thinks there is danger ahead so it will start pumping blood away from your stomach, so instead of walking, Larrys and Mindys get ready to flee and Sunnys and Yogis prepare to fight. If you consciously completely relax and bring the blood back to your belly, it helps turn your stress hormone back down to the appropriate level as you're saying to yourself, 'I'm relaxed enough to digest food right now. I'm not interested in fighting or fleeing.'

So before the lift doors even opened my client would be relaxed and breathing calmly. Then he needed to make sure his body language was open. To do this he had to hold his briefcase out in one hand and his laptop away from his body in the other hand, all the while thinking about projecting his big shiny belt buckle. By the time he calmly stepped out of the lift he would announce without saying a word, 'Here's Larry!' and everyone would take notice. Walking from the lift to the boardroom with long, slow, confident strides, instead of short, quick steps, would confirm his new relaxed, confident persona. It was so important that when he entered the room he put his laptop and briefcase on the table, quite a distance away in front of his chair, thereby claiming his space before he sat down. His arms must never sit on the inside of the arms of his chair; they must be placed on the arms themselves, and away from his body. Keeping your shoulders relaxed while you are opening up your upper body is essential when you are speaking to extroverted personalities. If you have tight shoulders at this stage, you will look defensive.

Before flying back overseas he spent quite a bit of time practising his new cowboy swagger, holding his briefcase and laptop away from his body and showing his belt buckle so that by the time he returned to the office his new body language was truly established. I got the most wonderful email from him. It simply said, *They listened to me!* I was so happy, as by gently rearranging his body language and radiating a confident assertiveness, he had gained the respect of his staff.

Another corporate gentleman I worked with had a strong Sunny temperament. He had quite a dominant personality, so the goal was to teach him to soften his approach – with people as well as horses. When you have a strong temperament with strong body language, you can come across intimidating to introverted temperaments. When he first started working with little Larry, Larry threw his head up, put his ears flat and ran backward, and the fellow hadn't even done anything! He couldn't understand why Larry had reacted to him that way, but to fix it was as simple as completely breathing out.

When people get angry and abusive, they hold their breath, so to a timid human or horse, if a strong personality is holding their breath it feels like they are going to do something in an aggressive manner. This triggers their flight instinct and they want to run away from that strong energy. Once the gentleman had relaxed his body language and breathed out completely, there were no more issues of him making Larry feel uncomfortable. It was quite a learning lesson for this fellow, as he finally figured out why his turnover of secretarial staff was so high! Once a strong Sunny personality understands that their strength is in their softness, it can be life changing not just for them but for their families and work colleagues. Most Sunny Cholerics are horrified when they realise that people close to them have felt intimidated by them.

I am distressed when I discover that people have felt intimidated in the workplace. No one in any circumstance should have to live with fear and intimidation. Everything I stand for here and everything I teach is to let people know that it is never acceptable to be bullied in any shape or form. It's not fair that certain personalities get victimised because they don't have the skills to stand up for themselves. They are usually the personalities that add a great deal to the workplace as they take the time to keep relationships intact. These relationships are so important as people spend more time with their work colleagues than they do with their own families. The number of beautiful, sensitive personalities I have seen get bullied and disrespected at work makes my blood boil.

Intimidation can be very subtle. It can be the tone of a voice or a disrespectful sideways glance or a slight shift in body language. Any of these can be enough to trigger anxiety in a sensitive person. It's especially important that young people in traineeship roles or starting out in their jobs are not intimidated while they are learning. Through our program I have helped many young people who started job training with so much enthusiasm and excitement but ended up with a bully as a manager or trainer, which stripped them of their confidence and dignity and forced them to leave the job.

One young girl had been through so much before she re-engaged with education, and then she worked hard to gain her qualification in child care. She absolutely adored children and finally to find a job doing what she loved was a dream come true for her. Within a few weeks her dream had turned to a nightmare as her training supervisor was so rude to her. She would speak down to her, snap at her and be so disrespectful that this young girl felt she had no choice but to leave the job. When I met her I was struck by her gentleness, which is such a special attribute to have when you are working in day care, as little children thrive with this motherly energy. She had lost all of her confidence and had decided she didn't want to put herself at risk like that again. As she progressed through the course, we talked a lot about how the bullying had started and how it had taken away her voice. She began to realise that her body shrank in front of her supervisor, which gave the woman more power. I encouraged her not to give up on her chosen career as she was a natural with children. We worked a lot on her puffing and popping and breathing out and relaxing, and before too long she regained her confidence to finish her placement hours at a different centre, where she is now flourishing.

Watching little Larry come onto our property and have to fit in with the clique that Sunny, Mindy and Yogi had when he arrived was quite difficult. He would try to fit in but they would just keep chasing him away. The way Larry handled it was to keep his own distance and appear pretty chilled most of the time. This led to Yogi wanting to come and make friends with him, as he was starting to look at him as a pretty chilled-out little dude. This is what I teach in my presentations – you don't need to try too hard to fit in anywhere, just make sure you relax and be yourself so that people learn to respect you for who you are, not for who you are trying to be. Little Larry could have gone in there kicking and squealing, pretending he was a real tough boy (which he so is not!) and he would never have got the respect he gained from just being himself. His acceptance into the herd came from him accepting himself, and as his own confidence grew, the other horses felt it too.

When you try to be somebody else just to fit in, people can always sense that it's not the real you. When you quietly stand your ground without trying to be loud or overconfident, people's respect for you will grow. It's always the calm, quiet confidence that builds respect in others as you are demonstrating respect for yourself when you display these qualities. And to think that it's working with horses that teaches us how to use these qualities to get the best outcomes.

CHAPTER 16

The depth and intelligence of horses never fails to amaze me. I'm convinced that Yogi, Sunny, Mindy and Larry know that what they are doing here is very special as there has never been a day, ever, in the eight years I have been running this program, that they have not been perfectly happy to work with every person who comes through our gate.

I believe our program has never at any stage put pressure on any of them, so they are always happy to do the work required. As with humans, if they had been treated disrespectfully, there would not have been the same willingness to participate in all the activities we ask of them.

Even though Sunny is a dominant horse, who thinks he knows what needs to be done when I'm riding him, when he is in the arena with the students he is like a different horse. Very nervous students feel intimidated by him at first, but he gently breathes on them and nuzzles the top of their hair as if he's reassuring them that he would never hurt them. Children as young as four, who are brought here by family services with their families, have attended our program and Sunny has worked at liberty with them. He will follow them anywhere, and as soon as they stop walking he instantly stops with them and nuzzles into their neck and breathes into their hair, which is strange because this is what mares do to their foals. It doesn't matter how many children step into the arena to have a turn with Sunny, he never gets tired of what he's doing and has exactly the same amount of affection and respect for every single student. Whether he's had a long day or it's raining or freezing cold or stifling hot, he is consistently gentle and respectful. I'm convinced he knows what he's doing. Young people's lives have begun to change in Sunny's presence. We have students who have been through horrific abuse. The trauma of those young people shows in their body language and demeanour. They arrive here looking crushed: no self-respect, full of fear and absolutely no confidence. To see them standing in front of Sunny looking so scared and lost and then to see Sunny drop his head and breathe on them to introduce himself and to let them know he's not going to hurt them is deeply moving.

When I teach these young students how to hold their body to ask Sunny to back away from them and he immediately listens to them and backs away, they can't believe it. They turn to me and say, 'He listened to me!' They can hardly believe it because they are not used to people hearing them. Over the sessions, their confidence grows before our eyes, until they are popping Sunny over jumps, getting him to circle them up to a canter with no rope on, and signalling for him to come in towards them and then adjusting their body language when he's close enough. By the end of their time with Sunny, it is almost as though they are different children.

Sunny even seems to know if someone has an injury. I had one girl who participated in my program whose arms were heavily bandaged from serious self-harm. At no time while she put him through the agility course did he come into her personal space or try to nudge her. With the student who came into the arena straight after her to do the same course, Sunny came in close and followed her with his nose literally on her shoulder. Without a doubt, Sunny knew that he needed to keep a safe distance from the girl with the heavily bandaged arms.

When we have our show presentation day, the students can dress up their horses in celebration. We have a big dress-up box of feather boas, top hats, bow ties, princess crowns and devil ears (for Yogi). I always laugh because the feather boas are meant to be for Mindy, but every show day, Sunny ends up being draped in pink and purple boas. He still continues to perform as a professional, even though I'm sure he's embarrassed!

Due to the lack of space here at our very small property, we often take Sunny, Yogi, Mindy and Larry with all of our students and our two dogs, our jump stands and jump poles and our agility markers, and food and drink down to the local park. We look like a travelling circus, all walking down the road together. Even in the huge park where there are no fences, students are able to take the rope off Sunny and work him at liberty with not a thought that he might run off and leave them. The students' confidence and happiness just beams out of them. Even experienced horse people are amazed at the level of horsemanship these young people display. It's because they've put their whole heart and soul into it. They've listened to every word I've said and followed every instruction because Sunny makes them feel so good about themselves. He is our amazing Teacher of Confidence.

If people watch Mindy out in the paddock with Sunny, Yogi and Larry they will notice that she keeps herself away from the boisterous behaviour at playtime. Mindy often wanders over to her room in the stables when the play gets rough. Like human melancholy temperaments, if Mindy was in a house where there was a lot of arguing she would go to her room and read a book, to stay away from it all, as melancholy Mindys avoid confrontation whenever they can.

Mindy has the ability to detect trauma and anxiety in the students. At the very first session with us, students sit in chairs around the arena watching me demonstrate with Sunny what they are going to learn over the next few weeks. It is amazing how Mindy will often wander over to a particular student and just start breathing on them, as a mare does to comfort her foal. It usually turns out that the child she has picked to nuzzle has been through the most severe trauma in the group. I think that as she is such a gentle pony, she is attracted to the same sort of gentleness and non-threatening temperament. If you were a new horse being put in the paddock, she would trot over and want to be friends with you if that's the sort of temperament you had. She would only trot over if there wasn't a Sunny or a Yogi in the paddock, as of course they are the main meeters and greeters.

Mindy feels safe with traumatised young people so she is very happy to be buddied up with them. She's almost like a mother figure to them. Mindy is very round and it doesn't matter how much we reduce her feed, she never changes shape. She is soft, round and incredibly cuddly. She is so soft that I often say to the students, 'When you cuddle Mindy, she feels like a fresh loaf of white bread that's just come out of the oven.'

One particular student I had matched up with Mindy had been through shocking abuse. The bond that this young girl developed with Mindy was absolutely precious. She and Mindy would spend so much time just cuddling. Mindy would turn her head and rest it against the girl's tummy, while the girl put her arms around Mindy's face, and they would stand there having a really special, affectionate time. It was as though Mindy was trying to make up for all the affection this young girl was missing in her life. The bond between Mindy and this girl grew very strong. Whenever Mindy saw her coming down the drive, she let out a loud nicker, which is unusual for Mindy, as she only usually nickers to tell me to hurry up when I'm mixing her dinner.

Mindy has a long flowing mane and the students love to brush it almost as much as Mindy loves it to be brushed. We will often be halfway through a session and Mindy will lead her human over to the brushes that are hanging on the fence to give them the hint, 'Forget about the work, how about you just brush my mane?' I use this as a great learning tool for teaching students to be assertive even when they feel sorry for somebody.

Mindy is the master manipulator. She'll look at the students with her big eyes and long eyelashes and all they want to do is say, 'Okay, Mindy. I'll just brush your mane. You don't have to do any work today.' But of course Mindy does need to work (it's not as if she has to do very much, she only has to trot in a couple of circles and pop over a jump). Even though Mindy makes them feel sorry for her they still have to firmly but gently ask her to go back into the work area and finish her tasks and then she will be rewarded with a brush at the end.

Mindy's beautiful mane has developed a session I call 'Plait and Chat'. There have been many occasions when a student and I have been plaiting Mindy's mane together, one of us on each side of her, and the youth worker leaning against the fence, and the student has opened up and revealed some very traumatic things that have happened or are happening to them, which they have never spoken about before. Plait and Chat creates a relaxed, non-judgemental space where students feel safe enough to reveal things they have kept silent about. When someone opens up they can then get professional help, which is the start of regaining their life.

In that safe environment students find the confidence to speak. Feeling like you have no voice can cause anxiety and depression. Feeling emotionally safe in relationships, whether they be personal or professional, is such an important aspect of life. I would like to see anxiety and depression be accepted in the same way a bad headache is: to be able to go into work and say, 'Gee I woke up with shocking depression (or anxiety) this morning.' This sort of acceptance will help stop people from feeling alienated.

Mindy is so soft and gentle as her mane is getting plaited and brushed. She closes her eyes and drops her head and projects such a gentle calmness that students also begin to feel relaxed and calm. Fortunately for Mindy as she's so lazy, she is very effective at her job without having to move much! So Mindy is truly the Queen of Nurturing.

Yogi is the complete opposite of Sunny, Mindy and Larry. He never takes his job seriously; he loses focus very quickly, gets incredibly bored and decides to go off and do his own thing. Yogi is all about entertainment with a capital E. I'll have students here who are very reluctant to participate in any way at the start of the program. They sit with folded arms and a sneer on their face, and then I present to them . . . 'Yogi!'

Usually I start with a flawless demonstration with Sunny working at liberty, running around me, doing a sliding stop when I request it, flying over jumps, walking sideways and backward with just the slightest cues from me. When it's time for Yogi, it's like he's been brought into math class when he hates math. When he's loose with all the horses in the paddock he's playful, he runs around very fast, in fact he yahoos. But the second I ask him to come into the arena, the head goes down, the feet drag and the attitude is, 'I'm at boring school.' My students with the folded arms and the sneers relate immediately and they start to giggle.

I then ask Yogi to start circling me at a trot and sometimes he just sits down. The giggles start to get louder. I ask him to get up on his feet and he will roll from side to side until he gets sick of it and finally decides to get up. Sometimes he lies down, stretches out flat and looks like he's gone to sleep. He will then lift one leg up a little bit higher because he likes getting his armpits scratched. By now, the arms have become unfolded, the students are sitting forward in their seats and they're actually laughing. I then ask Yogi to jump the jump for me, something Sunny and Larry have just demonstrated beautifully. He ambles over to the jump as he can't even be bothered to crank up the energy to move fast, and instead of jumping, he climbs up with his front feet and stands on the jump stand, looks at me and starts pawing the air asking for a scratch.

He is also fantastic at playing ball. I have a fit-ball in the paddock that is especially for Yogi. If I stand in front of him, quite a distance away, and roll it towards him, he will flick it back to me with his nose. We can play that for a very long time and I'm not sure which of us enjoys it the most. I put the ball in front of him and as the two of us run around together, he kicks and nudges the ball all around the arena as if we were playing soccer. However, at times during a session, Yogi will decide to trot off and start playing with his ball instead of focusing on what he is meant to be doing.

All these entertaining skills win over those students who don't want to participate. Yogi and I are quite a team at ice-breaking. Some might think that this is dreadful, disrespectful behaviour from a pony and it should be fixed. But Yogi and I have got the routine down pat. The most important thing is to engage these students who normally don't engage in anything.

It's as though Yogi has never grown up. He still loves playing; he still loves exploring. If anybody leaves a bag within reaching distance of Yogi through the fence, he drags it onto his side of the fence, opens it and scatters the contents everywhere to investigate what's inside. One youth worker was horrified as she had put her laptop bag where she thought it would be safely out of reach, but she'd underestimated how good Yogi is at getting hold of something he has his eye on. He managed to stretch himself far enough through the fence railings to grab the handle of the laptop bag, drag it into the paddock and run off with it, the laptop bouncing and bumping along the ground. As I saw him disappearing across the bridge to the other paddock, I called out, 'Yogi, stop right there!' He actually turned his head and looked at me before racing off at a speed that I can never get him to reach when I'm working him in the arena. Luckily once we retrieved the laptop from Yogi, it was unharmed thanks to the bag's thick padding.

The amount of caps, mobile phones, lunch boxes, water containers, paperwork and assorted personal belongings that have been spread across the paddock thanks to Yogi is innumerable. When Jake was at primary school and Yogi was still very young, Jake was walking down the drive one day after school when Yogi stole his schoolbag. He opened it easily and chewed

Jake's paperwork. When Jake went to school the next day and told the teacher that our pony had eaten his homework, she didn't believe him and I had to write him a note to explain that it was true!

One day I was delivering a team-building communication workshop to a group of psychologists from a large private practice. We have a rail across the bridge, which stops Yogi coming into the arena while I'm talking so that he doesn't distract people from what I'm saying. Sunny, Mindy and Larry are quite happy to stand quietly while I am talking, but not Yogi. On this particular day he was pushing his chest constantly onto the rail that was barring his entry. He had managed to snap the previous rail by constantly pushing into it and we had replaced it with a thicker one. I had finished explaining the other three temperaments and was now onto Yogi Sanguine, explaining that once they are determined to do something or get something, sanguines don't give up. I used Yogi's consistent pushing against the rail for the last half an hour as a great example of this.

One of the psychologists said to me, 'Well, he's not really that determined, because look, he's turned around and he's walking away.' I looked back and Yogi was heading towards the far end of the bridge. I said to her, 'This pony will not give up. He'll be back shortly.' Well, he was a great example of what a Yogi Sanguine personality is like when they're determined, as he got to the end of the bridge, turned around and faced the rail and launched into an extremely fast canter straight towards the rail. He rammed it with his chest at full speed and it snapped in half. He launched into the arena and ended up standing next to me as if nothing had happened! Everyone erupted in laughter.

Another time we had tried to keep him out of the arena by putting a piece of electric tape across the entrance. Yogi soon found out it wasn't really electrified and we were just bluffing. After pushing at it with his chest for quite a period of time, he realised he couldn't snap it. With absolute amazement, we watched him turn away from the tape, look over his shoulder, back himself up until his big fat hairy bottom hovered above the tape, and sit on it with all his weight to snap it. We were all in hysterics and it was absolutely brilliant timing as I had a group of students with me who found it hard to open up in any way. Yogi broke the ice and the energy shifted.

We have padlocks and so-called pony-proof locks on our gates, but Yogi can undo just about anything. We have a bolt on our stable door that goes down into the ground and it always has to be turned to the right so that Yogi cannot get his nose between the wall and the bolt. Sometimes if it is turned to the left, he will lift the bolt with his nose, turn it until it clicks into the unlocked position, slide open the door and let himself into the stable. It's not just to eat food, it's for his own amusement, as when this happens every rope, halter, brush bag, saddle cloth and container is pulled off shelves, off hooks or knocked over. The food remains untouched; it's the thrill of ransacking the room that he finds so entertaining.

Yogi always saves his breakouts for the middle of the night. The times I have been woken by Sunny screaming his head off, with the sound of hooves galloping back and forth across our wooden bridge because he is so stressed that Yogi has escaped. It's usually me in my pyjamas and a pair of gumboots and a torch who climbs through the fence into the neighbours' property, as of course the grass is always greener on the other side of the fence. Yogi loves these midnight escapades. He's such a problem to catch when he's out on a night-time adventure. He always runs over to me in our paddock but when he's out and about, just as I get close to him, he races off bucking and leaping, thinking it's wonderful. It usually takes a good half-hour before he gets bored with this hilarious game of watching his human run around someone else's garden in pyjamas and gumboots. He will then calmly walk over and let me know he's ready to come home. Meanwhile, Sunny is still screaming at the top of his lungs and waking up half the neighbourhood.

One particular day Yogi escaped as we were about to leave to go out. I said to Craig, 'No worries, I'll just pop him back in the paddock and make sure the gate is tied up as well as latched.' The neighbours had just put in a new garden bed and Yogi was happily exploring every little detail of it as if he were a landscape critic. Just as I got up to him, he shot off with one of his famous escape moves. Craig was sitting in the car watching the entertainment for a good fifteen minutes and gave the very helpful comment, 'Where are your horse whispering skills now?' I will leave it to your imagination what my response was, as I was all dressed up, with my heels getting stuck in the neighbours' new turf. My husband then stepped out of the car with one little gummy bear, whistled to Yogi, held up the tiny treat and Yogi trotted straight over, followed him down the drive and went straight back into his paddock. Thanks a lot, Yogi!

The bond I have with Yogi is hard to put into words. The love I have for him is so strong, not just because of what happened to his dad, which means I've always felt protective towards him (and funnily enough, Sunny has the same protectiveness with him), but also because of Yogi's ability to always make me laugh. Looking at him you would think he was just a scruffy-haired brown pony. You would have no idea of what an amazing personality lies under all that messy hair. He has a ponytail in the front because his mane is so long and scruffy, and he has a really long beard, which I'm tempted to put beads in! As soon as Yogi sees me, he always lets out the loudest nicker and comes racing over because he's always got so much to say. I have a little green plastic rake that comes from a child's beach set, which he loves me to scratch him with. When I walk away he darts in front of me to block my path and taps the ground, asking for more. My administration jobs get very much behind because I spend so much time scratching Yogi Bear's back.

In the paddock I have an old step box that I used to teach aerobics and his favourite thing to do is stand on it with his front legs. Often when I drive down our driveway I can see Yogi standing on that step, no one else around him; he's probably just feeling good because it makes him feel taller. When he's in an extra mischievous mood I'll have to say to him, as I'm pointing towards it, 'Go and stand on your step.' He goes straight over and stands on his step. He thinks it's making him the centre of attention, but it's actually just getting him out of our hair for a while!

Larry does an incredible job in the program. By being so amiable and friendly he melts the hardest of hearts. Every task he's asked to do, he does with such willingness and enthusiasm that the students can't thank him enough. In the arena, all four horses have their own specific area where they are tied up to be brushed before the session starts. When my volunteers arrive to help me get the horses and ponies ready, they go out into the paddock to catch them all. When it's Larry's turn to be caught, he is so funny as he walks away from whoever is trying to catch him and heads across the bridge all by himself and puts himself exactly in his place in the arena, as if to say, 'I know what's going on here, you don't need to catch me. I'm quite capable of getting into position myself.'

Larry is always so polite. At feed time, Sunny bangs his foot and pulls faces, even biting the rail in the stable. It's his way of saying, 'Hurry up, I want my dinner!' Yogi bangs buckets, pulls blankets off the rails, taps his foot continually and tries to undo the gate that leads into the feed shed. Mindy nickers constantly, just in case I've forgotten her, but Larry simply stands quietly, following me with his beautiful big eyes as if to say, 'When you're ready, I'll come and eat my dinner.' I've never seen him get agitated or be disrespectful. Unlike Yogi, who barges past if there is an opportunity ahead of either food or entertainment, Larry will quietly wait until he can walk on gently without disturbing anyone.

Larry's ability to bring out softness in some pretty hardened hearts has been nothing short of miraculous. Sometimes when I see the hardness in the students' eyes, I know it's there as a self-protection mechanism because they've been so hurt. The problem with leaving up this barrier, though, is that kind, gentle people have trouble getting through. Learning to trust again is challenging. You have to become vulnerable, and to many students that's terrifying. Larry allows them to drop their barriers without them ever feeling that they are going to be taken advantage of. This provides a small step towards helping them develop healthy boundaries instead of reinforced steel barriers.

Some students coming through our program have a problem containing their aggression and this has led them into all sorts of strife. Larry teaches them that when they are relaxed and soft, his respect for them increases in leaps and bounds. They learn that being soft is not the same as being weak. To see Larry go through his tasks for the students and then gently come in for a cuddle after he has completed each task, and to see these students come down to his level to thank him, never fails to bring a tear to my eye. Please note: these examples do not include dealing with violent or dangerous people. Please seek professional advice should you be involved with any physical or verbal abuse.

Another thing Larry teaches is never to underestimate someone because they are small. So many shy phlegmatic Larry humans get bullied. But when strong personalities get to know Larry and realise what a wonderful personality he has, they start to appreciate the friendships they can develop with people they sometimes wouldn't respect or make friends with.

CHAPTER 17

People imagine that I spend my days calmly drifting around
the paddock teaching people horsemanship skills, and they
think what a lovely peaceful working environment that would
be. It is a lovely environment, but on most days it's anything
but quiet and peaceful around here! On some days we will have
a minibus full of students and their youth workers, our volunteers and the work experience students all here at the same
time. Sometimes we can have up to twenty people for a single
session. Now, in that group of twenty we might have a mixture
of students with ADD, ADHD, Asperger's syndrome, social
phobia or oppositional defiance disorder, and I am telling you,
managing all of those different personalities is a challenge.

But it's a challenge I absolutely love with all my heart. Being able to make all the different personalities blend in, accept one another and work so well together is something that I look forward to every day.

My work experience students are extra special. They are the ones who have gone through the program and had amazing results and made changes in their lives. For them to come back and help other students deal with the issues they themselves have faced is so good for them. The more our work experience students help our new students, the more they grow in confidence and emotional strength. I am so proud of my special team as they have battled huge obstacles and are now able to help others on their journey. Many have returned to study as they finally have a clear vision of what they want to do with their lives. One has even gone to university to study counselling.

Keeping an eye on such a big group of students is a job in itself. On one particular day, we had gone into the stable to get all of the horses' brushes and halters to start the session. One of the students yelled out, 'Oh my god, is that a snake up there?' I said, 'Yes, that's our resident carpet snake, he lives in the stable rafters.' Now, I'm not a great fan of snakes, even though I love animals large and small. There's just something about snakes that makes me feel distinctly uncomfortable. Nothing against them or anything, but I think they ought to stick to their own habitat and not move into ours.

When I first saw our resident snake making himself at home on a rafter right above where I stand to mix up the horse feeds, I didn't cope with it very well. One of my students (a full-on Yogi Sanguine) told me that his dad worked with snakes and the whole family loved them and he was quite happy to take Mr Carpet Snake to their big property out in the valley, which was full of rainforest – beautiful carpet snake territory, you would think. He picked the snake up, much to my horror, and popped him into a huge bucket with a lid and very happily took Mr Snake out to join the rest of his family. It was a big relief to see Mr Snake exiting the property with a wildlife lover as I thought they would both be very happy with the arrangement.

Around two months later I said to one of the youth workers, 'You know, there's a snake on the same rafter the other one was living on and it's got exactly the same distinctive diamond markings.' She had been here the day I had first discovered Mr Snake, so she came down to the stables to have a look and informed me that it was in fact the same snake and it had come back. I said, 'You have got to be kidding me!'

She said, 'No, snakes are very territorial and clearly you need to take him further away.' He must have taken those two months to find his way back to my stable.

This time I got serious. I rang the snake expert (a snake whisperer). Again Mr Snake was removed from my rafter. He did not want to leave and wrapped his tail around the rafter very firmly, as if he were a squatter determined to stay. When the snake whisperer finally got Mr Snake into the bag, he assured me he would take him even deeper into the valley where it's a wonderful habitat for snakes, much nicer than my barren, dusty stable. So I happily watched Mr Snake exit the property for the second time.

A couple of months after that, he was back. When I rang another snake whisperer, he informed me that you usually have to take them over a couple of creeks before they lose the scent of where to come back to. By this stage I realised that I just had to accept this snake because he was going to keep on coming back. I decided I had to overcome my fear of snakes. I upturned a bucked and stood on top of it so that my head was level with Mr Snake. 'Okay,' I told him, 'I accept that you've moved back in and I'm going to try to get used to you being here every day.' He lifted his head, turned and looked at me, his tongue flickering, and it gave me such a fright that I fell off the bucket. I moved all of my feeding paraphernalia so that I didn't have to ever stand under that rafter again. You may be thinking, what a wuss, but remember I was brought up in the South Island of New Zealand. I learnt to handle earthquakes and freezing weather conditions but I never had to deal with snakes, cockroaches or big spiders!

I tried not to mention the snake to my students; I thought it was better than they didn't know about it. Often they would stand under that rafter and have no idea there was a huge carpet snake a few inches above their head. But some days, while I was in the arena, I would hear shrieks coming from the stable as someone who had been sent over there to get a bucket or a brush had caught sight of Mr Snake.

One particular session there was a young girl who was fascinated by snakes. She told me that she had a pet snake at home and asked could she please pick up Mr Snake. I said, 'Absolutely no way, because he's not a pet, even though he's moved in and thinks he's part of the family. He's not used to being handled and for the sake of everyone's nerves, please leave him where he is.'

Not five minutes later, when my back was turned, she called my name and said, 'Look!' She was waving his head towards me, his tail in her other hand, and she was making a really loud hissing noise and then laughing. I said, 'Put that snake down right now! By the way, those words should not even be coming out of my mouth!' All the other students were by this time screaming and shrieking while the youth worker tried to remove Mr Snake from the girls' arms and pop him back up onto his rafter.

Although what I love the most is being in the paddock with my horses and students, my world has grown beyond that now and I find myself in all sorts of unexpected roles promoting the work we're doing. I'm often asked to be a keynote speaker and to give talks at schools or organisations, and there are always enquiries from television, newspapers and magazines for interviews.

This year, due to cuts in government funding to the youth sector, we have had to find alternative ways of keeping ourselves going. The government cuts have meant that a lot of youth organisations that would normally have the funds to bring students to our program now don't have access to the money or, even worse, have closed down and their remarkable youth workers made redundant. I had never heard of crowd funding until one of my psychology placement students noticed how hard it was for us without sufficient funding. She said to me, 'I'd love to help organise a crowd funding campaign for you.' She explained that crowd funding sites allow you to tell your story via video and explain why you need funds. Word is spread through social media and people are able to donate money to your cause. The fact that this young woman came along at the exact moment I most needed her help was a miracle in itself.

The posting of our crowd-funding video online has created a whirlwind of interest as everyone wants more information about our program, which is fabulous. As I write this, I'm preparing for a crew from a well-known television show to come and film a segment here. The horses all seem to love the camera as they are on their best behaviour as soon as film crews arrive. Yogi especially loves the fluffy sound boom and it has to be held up very high so that he can't grab it.

All this means that life is incredibly busy and, if I am honest, I have struggled to maintain balance and have at times been very unwell. Over the years I have often literally run myself into the ground, simply because I haven't known how to slow down. I would try and try not to cram my days with activity, but no matter how hard I tried, I would always get swept up in a whirlwind of busyness again. At last, though, I have finally understood why I've never been able to slow down.

I have recently been diagnosed, after having a battery of assessments, with ADHD. It now makes sense why I can understand and communicate so well with the students who come here, and this is because I struggled, as they do now, when I was younger. I fully understand what they are feeling and how hard it is for them to be still and focus. It's still hard for me! It's amazing how quickly students with ADD, ADHD and Asperger's syndrome can connect with horses. They have a natural sensitivity that helps them relate to animals.

Being diagnosed with ADHD has helped me understand myself a lot better. I've struggled for years trying to make my brain work in a structured and organised way (you should see my handbag and my desk!) and have judged myself for not being what I classed as normal. I now realise that it's not normal to try to do twenty things in a day without allowing myself travel time, eating time or resting time, although I'm not always good at remembering this.

Some people think that you can't be successful if you have ADHD. I've proven them wrong and have been able to teach many, many others how to reclaim their lives and rebuild their confidence. It's incredibly empowering for people with ADHD to realise that they can still achieve goals and be successful in their lives. What I have observed over the last few years is that once people diagnosed with ADD or ADHD find a passion for something, they can excel.

Around this time I also discovered that I had gastritis, which is an inflammation of the stomach lining and can be the precursor to an ulcer if not treated, as well as many food intolerances and allergies. I spent months going from specialist to specialist as things kept going wrong all over my body. If it wasn't for the great team at a wellness clinic here on the Gold Coast and my doctor who referred me for blood and urine tests, the dots would never have been joined. Together those dots make up Pyrrole Disorder.

When you have a lot of stress and illness in your life, the oxygen-carrying molecule in your blood, haemoglobin, produces excessive amounts of the waste byproduct hydroxy-hemopyrrolin-2-one (HPL), also known as pyrrole. HPL binds to the nutrients zinc, vitamin B6 and biotin, so they cannot be absorbed in your body and are instead excreted through your urine. Both zinc and B6 play an important role in behaviour and mood control, our ability to handle stress, our feelings of happiness and our capacity to learn. Zinc and B6 play a part in the production of the neurotransmitters serotonin and gamma-aminobutyric acid (GABA), which have regulatory effects on your mood. Normal levels of serotonin and GABA facilitate calmness, stability and an ability to deal with stress. It is thought that Pyrrole Disorder can play a role in ADD, ADHD, anxiety and depression. Through very high doses of vitamins and an amino acid, methionine, compounded by a pharmacist, symptoms can be greatly reduced.

I've thought a lot about discussing my journey with depression and anxiety in this book, but it's impossible to tell the story of my relationship with horses without acknowledging how crucial they've been to my emotional wellbeing. From a very young age I turned to horses when I was feeling low or needed calming down and they gave me comfort. This has been true throughout my adult life too. All the people I've worked with over the years in the fitness industry and in the business I run now would never have had any idea how much I have struggled with anxiety and depression. When you put on a happy face all the time, no one knows how you're really feeling; when you hit extreme lows people don't understand why you seem to be withdrawing from them, or they think you're too busy to contact them.

Getting so rundown and overcommitting myself triggered my anxiety to a level I hadn't reached for quite a few years.

Lots of visits to specialists, doctors and hospitals (I was taken by ambulance to hospital twice within a couple of months due to my stomach problems), plus keeping the charity running and meeting all my other work commitments pushed my stress levels over the limit. When your health is good you can handle added pressure, but as soon as your health is compromised, your tolerance to stress plummets. When I look back I can see I was so busy running the charity that I was missing out on my own time with my horses. I didn't make time to take Sunny for rides or to the beach, and even taking the ponies to the park for a quiet nibble on the grass, which was something I used to love, was not happening because I was so busy.

I discussed my rising anxiety with my doctor. She advised me to take a break. I told her I couldn't take a break right then because as well as writing this book I had a full schedule of youth and family organisations sending students to us, TV crews booked in, various media interviews and guest-speaking functions to attend, and I had just heard that I had been nominated for a Gold Coast Women in Business Award (which was an absolute honour and very exciting!). She shook her head and said, 'What you actually need is three weeks in Thailand at a special retreat so that you can relax *properly* with no phone or internet.'

I said, 'I can't, I've got no time.' The famous last words that always lead to trouble.

Within a few weeks I was back again saying that my anxiety was even worse. I was not sleeping and my heart was pounding most of the day, even when I wasn't being active. My doctor asked me again, 'Have you had a break?' I repeated, 'I've got no time!' I really hope that someone reading this will learn a lesson before they go through what I've been through and take the advice from experts when they are told to have a break. My stress levels were so high that I couldn't bring them down with my usual relaxation techniques.

After a blood test showed that my immune levels were very low, my doctor suggested I go to a local private clinic that specialised in anxiety. By this stage Craig had come with me to my appointment as he didn't trust me to tell the doctor how bad a state I was really in.

When you suffer from gastritis and reflux and food intolerances and allergies (all caused by stress, mind you), your whole body feels like it's breaking down. Everything you eat makes you nauseous and lethargic. You constantly feel like you have a virus or food poisoning. The nausea was unremitting, as was my anxiety. I felt so ill I was prepared to try anything, so I rearranged my bookings (for those of you who think you can't do this, you actually can); organised someone to look after my special horsey family, and booked myself into the clinic.

As my doctor had earlier mentioned a retreat in Thailand, I was expecting the clinic to be a similar sort of thing. Well, when I got there I realised it was a small hospital that specialised in anxiety, depression and addictions, with each disorder having its own ward. As soon as I walked in I said to the lovely lady who greeted me, 'I'm sorry, I can't stay here. I visualised it as something entirely different and I just can't handle staying in a hospital environment.'

She was probably quite used to this kind of response, so she took me down to show me the anxiety ward, which did have a lovely courtyard, but when she showed me my room, I realised I couldn't open the window. Off I went again, as I am incredibly claustrophobic. Even in winter I have all the windows and doors wide open and all the curtains pulled back. I can't sit in rooms without windows for very long or even stay in hotels where you can't open the window. So it was no surprise that I said to the lady, 'I'm sorry, I can't possibly stay here. I can't open the window and I can't see any trees!' My anxiety was getting worse and worse. I didn't know what to do. My nausea was rising, the pains in my stomach were intensifying and my anxiety was so high I felt like I was going to pass out. I knew I had to have this break to get my health back on track but I could not stay in that room.

I started negotiations. 'How about I stay next door in a unit so at least I will have a view and be able to open my window at night and I can attend the clinic's program on a daily basis?' Her response was that she had to ask the director, as it was not a usual request; most people were happy with the room they were given. Permission was granted and I was able to attend the in-patients program while staying 'out'. Where I stayed,

I could see the ocean, so it was wonderful. I'd wake up and have breakfast watching the waves and then walk through parkland to the clinic.

The level of education in the clinic was fantastic. I was once again reminded about mindfulness, meditation, boundaries and time management, everything I'd let go out the window recently. I did not want any student to miss out on the opportunity to attend our program, so I had got into the habit of forgetting to block out my diary for important things like eating and resting! I certainly wasn't leaving any time for myself or for my own 'horsey time'. I had spent the last few years giving every ounce of myself to other people and I didn't have a drop left.

To sit and be taught instead of being the teacher was something I appreciated so much. The staff were nurturing and understanding and they helped me to work out why I had got myself into such a bad state. I met some beautiful people in the anxiety group, people from all walks of life and careers, and it really hit home to me that we don't have any idea about what is going on inside another person.

I have learnt to be conscious that any problems or issues I have do not define me. True, they are a part of who I am, but they are not the whole story. The way I like to explain it to my students is to ask them to imagine their life flowing along on two separate train tracks, side by side. On one track is your essence, your being, your goals, your dreams, people who are close to you. On the other track is whatever hardships are happening at that time. It is so important to keep the hardships on their own track so that you don't become immersed in them and your life can keep flowing forward and your true self does not become defined by the difficulties you are facing. In this way, the tracks run parallel and allow growth and hope to keep developing.

While I was attending the clinic I found out that I had reached the finals of the Gold Coast Women in Business Awards for Community Dedication. I was absolutely thrilled and felt incredibly honoured. Of course nobody knew the state I was in. If they did, they would have understood that receiving the news was such a joy when I was at my absolute lowest.

The psychiatrist I was seeing in the clinic didn't prescribe any medication as he said overcommitting and over-cramming were the crux of the problem. In addition, being overwhelmed by the financial stress involved in trying to keep the charity afloat, I'd forgotten to do all the things that made me feel relaxed and calm. Like spending quality time by myself with my beautiful ponies and Sunny.

At my first appointment with my psychiatrist, I was very nervous about going in to speak to someone I hadn't met before as I felt embarrassed to be in such a state. This was absolutely ridiculous as I'd been helping people every day who felt like I did now and I had never once judged them, so I should have realised that he wouldn't judge me either. It's just it was such a shock to realise that my body and mind had reached a limit. I thought I was invincible, with endless energy and motivation, and that I would always be able to go at a furious pace. So there I was, sitting and talking to him so earnestly and trying to learn how to de-stress when suddenly the fire alarm went off. It was so loud we were shouting at each other across the desk. He said it should stop soon as they'd been having some problems with the alarm. The next thing, an incredibly loud voice said, 'Evacuate the building! Evacuate the building!' over and over again. The psychiatrist shouted over the din, 'Do you mind if we go outside? It should stop soon.' I shouted back, 'I'd love to go outside,' thinking to myself that I was always much happier outdoors anyway. We settled down on the edge of a small retaining wall and launched straight back into the conversation we'd been having inside (the alarm was still going off very loudly in the background). The next thing we knew, the fire brigade turned up and reversed into the area we were sitting in. Firemen jumped out of the fire engine, interrupting our talk yet again. I said to myself, 'What a typical start for me when I've come to an anxiety clinic to learn to relax!' My sense of humour kicked in then and I couldn't stop laughing. It was really nice because the psychiatrist and I were having a good laugh together and it made me feel comfortable to start off on that footing.

The afternoon of my first day finished with a yoga session that included a deep meditation. There we all were, all of us from the anxiety group, lying on our yoga mats and desperately trying to relax because it didn't come naturally to any of us. The yoga instructor took about twenty minutes with our breathing and our relaxation before he was satisfied that we were actually starting to relax. I was thinking at the time, 'Oh, okay, I can do this. I can lie still. I can chill out.' Someone next to me had started to snore and I was jealous as I would have liked to have been as instantly relaxed as that. Well, you wouldn't believe it, all of a sudden the fire alarm went off again. The shock made everybody pop up and we looked like a room full of meerkats that have sensed danger!

I finished the program with my anxiety at a much lower level. I had been reminded of the coping strategies I needed to use: stopping during the day and doing some mindfulness and meditation; structuring my day better; saying no when I was exhausted rather than, 'Yeah that'll be fine.' However, as my anxiety levels dropped, another issue emerged. I developed depression like I have never had in my life. I felt completely flat and everything seemed to have lost its lustre.

My energy was so low I had to drag myself everywhere. Helplessness and sadness were overwhelming. Because my stress levels had been so high for so long, they had actually disguised the depression. Trying to stick to a regular routine, staying positive, things that I would normally do naturally, were now such an effort. My doctor explained that this was quite normal as my anxiety and stress and health were at such a detrimental level that I had swung like a pendulum from anxiety to depression. She also explained that I was meant to be slowing things down but not stopping them completely as my personality needs to be purposively active. I was trying to sit still and just relax but I needed to learn the balance of being active, having goals and achieving them without running myself into the ground.

In time I learnt that balance. I am quite aware, though, that if I allow myself to become almost manic with busyness and push myself too far I will very quickly upset that balance.

Everyday now when I start to get frantic with activity I take myself down to the paddock to see Sunny and the ponies. Larry seems to have assigned himself the role of de-stressing Sue as when I sit down near the stables, he comes and snuggles against me. He can only do that when Yogi has food, though, otherwise Yogi pushes him out of the way, and after Mindy has ambled over to see me and then ambled back to her favourite shade tree. I sit there for about fifteen minutes and slowly the world stops spinning around me. I make time for breaks so I can eat properly and instead of dashing about while grabbing handfuls of food as I go, I block out a lunchtime – normal for some, but in the past I'd keep going until evening.

When your days are so busy it's important to use your breaks as mini meditations. It only takes fifteen minutes of conscious stillness (no phones, no computers, no chatting!) and I literally feel my body reset itself to a slower speed.

After eating (slowly!) you can just sit, breathing slowly and deep and listening to the birds or the wind in the trees. If you're working inside, a nature cd is perfect and you can listen out for particular noises, birds, water running or the sound of waves. For all you frantic personalities (like mine), understanding you are not a machine but a complex sensitive being who needs to connect to nature can make such a difference to your daily life.

I encourage my corporate clients who spend so many hours in their workplace to take the time out after work, if possible, to walk through a park or near some water, and on the weekends to spend time outside with their families so that they can feel reconnected with the beauty and energy that is around us, to take the time to look for it and feel it. It really makes a difference.

CHAPTER 18

So there I was, one week out of the clinic, getting organised to attend the Gold Coast Women in Business Awards for 2014 at the Palazzo Versace. In that week leading up to the awards I had two high schools start the program, some family groups come for workshops and also more media interviews – and I was trying very hard to take things slowly (that was slow for me!).

The day of the awards arrived and I was full of excitement because just to be nominated was such an honour. I had organised the morning with absolute precision, starting with the hairdresser at eight o'clock. I turned up at ten to eight, which astounded me because I have always had a problem with time management and was usually late. So see, I had learnt from the clinic! Eight o'clock came around and the salon still wasn't open. I had made the appointment for eight o'clock to allow enough time to get ready and to make it to the function on time. So by ten past eight I was becoming very anxious. I was sitting in the car, frantically doing my deep breathing to 'stay calm, stay calm, stay calm', when someone turned up and opened the doors. Much to my horror, it wasn't my hairdresser. She said to me, 'Oh, we've got you booked in for eight-thirty. There must have been a mix-up with the times.'

One of my psychology placement students had organised her mum, who was a make-up artist, to do my make-up. I'd never been nominated for anything like this before, so I was going all out. I was meant to be home by nine, but of course I was late. It was a humid day and the make-up artist said, 'Don't worry, we'll get it done. Just stay cool inside and we'll get you finished in time.' I had organised someone else to attend to the horses that morning, so I didn't have to go out in the paddock and get dirty and sweaty. I felt, for a change, rather immaculate; I'm usually covered in sunscreen, dust and pony hair.

Everything was going well, then I looked out the window to see Yogi had escaped and was in the neighbours' paddock with their pet cow. Oh no, I thought. Now I had to go out there, catch him, bring him home, fix the fence and sort out the electric fence as well, to make sure he doesn't get out again. Next thing, I'm out in the paddock, Yogi took a look at me, stuck his tail in the air and must have thought, *No way am I going home, the grass is too good here*, and proceeded to fang around the paddock with the cow in pursuit. After I'd done three circuits of the paddock after him, he decided to trot over to me and follow me home. Problem was, he was leaning his dirty, sweaty body up against my lovely clean, moisturised, ready-for-the-function body, and I was trying to push him away, saying, 'Get off me, Yogi!'

The make-up artist was horrified. She said, 'What are you doing out there? You've got to come in and finish getting ready.' I finally got Yogi settled and the fence fixed and returned inside to repair the damage of frizzed hair and sweaty horse smell.

I was sitting on the make-up stool, clean again, with a fan blowing on me, thinking *Okay, here we go. We might be running behind schedule but it's all good now*, when I got a phone call from Craig, who was taking me to the awards, to tell me that he had a flat battery and was waiting for roadside assistance. Well, up went my anxiety again. The make-up artist was telling me to breathe, my heart was pounding, I was thinking, *Of all days*. Craig finally returned home, got ready in about five minutes (as men can) and in a flurry of action we jumped in the car and were finally off.

After all that, we actually got there on time! The Palazzo Versace was such a beautiful setting for the awards, which were held in the hotel ballroom. It was attended by federal and state ministers, councillors, city leaders, media and special guests. The prestigious Gold Coast Women in Business Awards is run by Karen Phillips. She is an amazing mentor for women and her passion for encouraging and uniting women is inspirational. The award recognises and honours exceptional women making a difference to our city, the Gold Coast.

As we were enjoying our lunch, they began calling up the three finalists for each category. When they got to the Community Dedication award, I was thinking to myself how exciting it was for those who had reached the final three. I never imagined I was going to be one of them! They called out the first finalist's name to go up on stage and I was clapping and eating my meal at the same time when, shock and surprise, my name was called next. I nearly choked on my lunch and Craig was saying, 'That's you, off you go!' Walking up to the stage was a blur; it felt totally surreal because I had not been expecting it. Up on stage, the room looked huge and filled with so many people. They called up the third finalist and we were all busy shaking each other's hands, just excited to be up there, and I was just thinking, *How great is this, I'm a finalist, how amazing.*

Then the announcement was made, 'The winner of the 2014 Women in Business Award for Community Dedication is Sue Spence.' I was so shocked, my hands flew up to cover my face and my eyes popped out like ping-pong balls and that's when the official photo was taken!

It was incredibly humbling to be given the award when the other finalists were remarkable women doing outstanding work in the community. You certainly don't do this sort of work to gain accolades. You work in quite an isolated way really. Most people aren't aware of what you're doing, only those you are working with, most of whom are in extreme need. To be recognised by the Gold Coast Women in Business Awards gave me a feeling of being part of something a lot bigger. I felt I was part of the whole community and that I was supported by a team working together to make our community better.

The award has made Gold Coast businesses aware of what I do, which has made it easier to promote the needs of our charity locally. It has also highlighted what I do at a corporate level, with the popular team-building workshops, communication coaching and motivational speaking. All of which help support the charity. All this is essential to help get the Horse Whispering Youth Program's PowerPoint program and Educational Workshops in as many schools and youth services as possible, so that everyone can learn about their temperament, as well as other people's; understand about anxiety, depression and bullying; learn effective body language skills, empathy and most importantly self-respect and respect for all. This will ensure that as many people as possible can access the skills they need to thrive, no matter what their background or self-perceived limitation.

Recently I attended a women's retreat to try to help me slow down. I heard a phrase there that I've never heard before:

'Feather, brick, truck.' What this means is when you get a little warning (feather) that you're doing too much or ignoring a niggling medical issue, if you don't listen to the feather you will then be hit by a brick. So the stress or the symptoms will get worse. If you continue to ignore the brick, at some stage you are going to be hit by a truck. So you'll blow a fuse or become ill and have no alternative but to stop everything you are doing to try to regain your health and your sanity.

I look back over the years and realise I never listened to feathers or bricks, it was always the trucks that got me! Leading up to my breast cancer diagnosis, my stress levels were sky high. My days were crammed full from the second I opened my eyes to the second I closed them again and tried to sleep (of course, thanks to my high stress levels, I had insomnia). When I was hit by the truck, in the shape of breast cancer, it was a massive wake-up call. When you have no choice but to sit still in a hospital bed because you've had major surgery, you realise that the world goes on without you trying to control every part of it.

You would have thought that being hit by that big truck, I would have learnt my lesson to slow down, but a few months after my reconstruction was completed, I started to feel back to normal again and off I went. Back to cramming things in, back to rushing around. I just could not stop myself from slipping back into race mode. I was having spells of dizziness as I wasn't completely recovered from surgery. My body had been through so much but I pushed the fatigue away (the feather) and thought, *Come on, just get on with it.*

I remember one night the dizziness was getting a lot worse (feather) but I still raced off after a busy day to teach an aerobics class. As I was lying on the couch that night completely exhausted, I started to hear a loud ringing in my ear. It got louder and louder (brick) but I ignored it. It continued ringing incredibly loudly the next morning. I again pushed the brick aside as I had lots of things to do.

That night the ringing grew even louder, and when I woke up the next morning and tried to get out of bed, the truck drove straight into me and I fell over. I had lost my balance and the ringing in my ear was unbearably loud. The truck I had been hit with was called labyrinthitis. It's a virus that attacks the inner ear. I ended up losing hearing in my right ear and instead of hearing, I had tinnitus, which is so loud I can't hear out of my good ear properly anymore. I always have to let my students know that if they have anything to say to me, they must come and stand on my left side so that I can hear them. It's actually rather stressful because people can't tell when you can't hear properly, so I'm always trying to adjust my body to hear their words and they just think I'm fidgeting! A lot of the time my brain goes 'sounds like' and I'll answer a question that's got nothing to do with what I've actually been asked.

That truck slowed me down for a few months as I couldn't believe I'd lost my hearing and I had this horrendous ringing in my ears. But after a few months, off I went again! I was actually getting busier than ever. I was still working part time in the gym, teaching aerobics, and I'd just started my Horsemanship program with the students. I was starting to get some niggling pain in between my shoulder blades, which I ignored (feather). I couldn't work out why because I couldn't recall pulling any muscles. It proceeded to get worse (actually really quite painful – brick), but I was too busy to go to the doctor until one day I collapsed. I was hit by the truck, then delivered by ambulance to Emergency and diagnosed with cholecystitis (inflammation of the gall bladder). I didn't have gallstones, just an incredibly badly infected gall bladder and I had to have immediate surgery to remove it.

You would have thought that after three major illnesses within a short space of time I would be making some serious changes in the way I lived my life. But again, off I went like a runaway train.

I then started to get some stomach pain (feather). By now I was sick of going to doctors and hospitals so I pushed it aside. Again the pain got worse (brick), until one day it was so bad, it dropped me to the floor like a stone and I could not get up because the pain was so acute. Again, the truck had arrived and again off I went by ambulance to the same hospital. This truck carried a burst ovarian cyst.

Have I mentioned how expensive these trucks can be? It's like the lines from 'An interview with God' where God was asked, 'What surprises you most about mankind?' and one of

God's answers was 'that they lose their health to make money and then lose their money to restore their health'.

As my doctor pointed out recently, because I'd been through breast cancer and a double mastectomy, I fobbed off all these other, more minor health issues, but now I realise that, if left untreated, they can be just as serious. So there I was, missing two boobs, a gall bladder, the hearing in my right ear, and an ovary, and I was still not learning my lesson.

Changes were desperately needed. I had friends who had never been to hospital in their lives and for me it was becoming a regular occurrence. This was when my Natural Horseman-ship started to impact positively on my health. Working with Sunny at liberty on a regular basis was making me stay in the moment. It stopped my thoughts from racing ahead. When your thoughts race ahead, your body ends up racing with it. It's like permanently living in an express train going three hundred kilometres per hour. You go racing past stops with your hands and face pressed up against the window, saying to yourself, 'Gee, I wish we could have stopped there. I'd love to go back and have a look at that place.' But you know you're never going to make the time to stop and get out of the train and enjoy the places you've seen go flashing by. I want my life to be like the Puffing Billy. It puffs up through the ranges, slowly and surely, but you can open the windows wide, lean out the window and pick a flower on the way and enjoy the journey.

Some days when I start to speed up I will watch Mindy grazing in the paddock, slow and relaxed, or dozing under her tree, and it's as though I tune in with her unhurried, reassuring energy and physically feel the wound-up energy I'm carrying slowly unwind. Living with ADHD can feel like three or four television sets are playing in my head at the same time, and they're all on different channels. Being able to work with horses literally tunes my mind into one TV and one channel only, the Horse Channel! This is the channel that operates from a place of such grounding that all of my potential can be expressed.

What I have observed working with a lot of adults is that the ones who become workaholics and are constantly pushing themselves to achieve and never take the time to relax actually push themselves to a state very similar to a person who has ADHD. Their brain is constantly jumping from one thing to the next. They are always on high alert and their adrenal glands are always working overtime, which leads to adrenal fatigue. It is in this state that feathers and bricks are never paid attention to, and too often the only thing that slows some people down is a truck. It is at this point that most people reassess the way they are living their lives. My message here is don't wait for the truck in order to start reassessing, as some trucks won't give you the chance – they'll knock you down and you might not get up again. Make the changes now. Slow down and appreciate what is really important in your life. It is possible to have a balance of work, family and relationships.

CHAPTER 19

Ever since I was a little girl I have known that horses make my heart sing. It is only now, after many of life's ups and downs, that I realise how important it is for all of us to have something that makes our heart sing. Something that brings us happiness, or peace, or delight. Some people dance, some play musical instruments; some people meditate or do yoga, and some play sports. For me, it's horses.

This connection is something that fills my heart and spirit.

When you are with or even around horses, a part of you connects with an energy that is almost mystical. There is a stillness within their majestic energy that seems to project wisdom and dignity. They have such strength, but within that strength is softness; they can give you playfulness and then in other instances give you calmness and peace.

I recently had the privilege to meet and ride a warmblood-cross-Clydesdale showjumper that was over seventeen hands high. He was so big my head only came halfway up his shoulder. When he put his head up, I couldn't even reach it. After being around my beautiful Sunny and my wonderful ponies, he seemed like a giant. Yet when he lowered his head all he wanted to do was gently nuzzle me. The term 'gentle giant' is not enough to express the feeling you get when something so big and strong demonstrates such soft gentleness. It makes you look at the world through different eyes. It makes you look for the good, not just in horses but in people; it makes you look for the softness that is in there behind the hardness. I realised that the old saying 'don't judge another by their appearance' is so true.

I have recently returned from New Zealand. Being back in the places I used to ride – the countryside, the forests, the beach I used to gallop Lady along – made me realise how incredibly lucky I was to have such beautiful surroundings to grow up in, with no hustle and bustle and nothing to interfere with the energy that comes from connecting to nature. I realise now that when I used to ride Lady through the pine forests I was prac-tising mindfulness without knowing it. To be in the cocooning silence of the forest, with only the sound of birdsong, the groan of swaying pine trees and, in the far distance, the sound of the ocean, to be sharing that peaceful environment with the horse that I loved with all my heart was a rare gift.

That trip made me remember the joyful excitement Lady and I felt when we galloped up to the top of the sandhills and down onto the beach. I could feel the freedom and joy resonating between the two of us. To be able to experience these moments, even during the times when I was struggling with anxiety or being bullied, was God-given medicine. Even the quiet ride back would lull me into a state of calmness as Lady's long, smooth strides took me safely home.

When you are walking along slowly on a horse or pony, completely in tune with them, it's almost hypnotic. I love it now when Sunny and I take a quiet ride around the area where I live. I remember right back to my riding lessons with Bracken when I was little, when we were allowed to amble around the big paddock surrounded by pine hedges. I used to love just hearing the clip clop, clip clop of Bracken's hooves as he plodded along the track carpeted with pine needles.

In the world of horses you're fully immersed in the moment. I can't even begin to describe how beautiful it is when I'm sitting in the paddock with my loving white Shetland pony Mindy as she softly nuzzles my hair and breathes on me with such a nurturing gentleness. When Yogi runs over and starts rolling his ball towards me or standing on his stool and asking me to scratch him or even when he steals my hat off my head, he makes me laugh and feel joyful. I feel such pride when Sunny stands strongly by my side. He projects calm assurance to me, as he does to his herd of ponies that he protects so well. And the look on Larry's face when he very gently approaches me, almost as if he's asking permission for a cuddle, fills my heart to the brim.

To think that all of my relationships and experiences with horses throughout my life, and all the ups and downs I've experienced have merged together to form the program I now teach is nothing short of amazing.

My mind boggles when I think of how my little herd came together and then touched the lives of thousands of people. The recognition, even internationally, for the program has been amazing. It has always been my dream that Horses Helping Humans™ and my charity, the Horse Whispering Youth Program, would be available all over Australia and New Zealand, so that it would be accessible for young people who need the help. That dream has now become a reality. Horses Helping Humans™ has become a licensed program and I am now busy compiling manuals, making business plans and training licensees to open centres just like this one. I want to make it possible for others with horsemanship and people skills to have the opportunity to help young people in their local communities, so that many more lives can be touched. Meeting with trademark, intellectual property and licensing lawyers has really brought home to me how far my program has come. Now, there could be centres like mine opening up all across Australia – what an amazing feeling! And to think all this started with just me and my horses, in a small dusty paddock. I'm so blessed.

I have also trademarked my brand, Sue Spence Communications, so look out for this brand (SS) on all Horses Helping Humans™ websites, literature and all social media, to be assured that my original program is being delivered.

I am not a horse trainer, or a specialised riding instructor, or even a horse whisperer. I refer people with problem horses to amazing Natural Horsemanship clinics. If I am to be identified as anything, I would like to be known as a people whisperer! The gift I have of being able to read people and understand where they are coming from and then to teach them how to connect with and respect one another is something I appreciate on a daily basis. There are now thousands of people worldwide practicing Natural Horsemanship, which has created a much better world for horses, a world filled with trust and respect.

I would like to say thank you to all my students from the bottom of my heart as, without realising it, they have helped me by allowing me to help them. Some of them, when they were at rock bottom, wouldn't have imagined how they could possibly have helped anyone. But by accepting help, they have given me my purpose in life. My hope for them all is that they live their lives with respect, trust, acceptance and dignity.

I can honestly say every horse and pony I have had since I was young has helped me in myriad ways. Blackie, Bracken, Judy, Sandy, Lady, Socks, Scooby, Sunny, Yogi, Mindy and

Larry have added so much joy to my life. They've helped give me confidence and shown me how to appreciate the simple things in life, like just sitting and enjoying being connected with them. This has helped me learn to sit and enjoy the other beautiful things that nature has to offer us. They have taught me that the most important thing in life is acceptance and trust.

Every day I feel deep gratitude in my heart for the privilege of having horses in my life.

ACKNOWLEDGEMENTS

My heartfelt thanks go to some amazing people, whose generosity has kept the Horse Whispering Youth Program charity running. Daniel and Danielle, you have been responsible for the growth of the program, allowing us to help thousands of young people and families. Peter and Alison, for funding students who would not have been able to attend and for being a part of making a massive change to their lives.

To Ishka, your generosity has supported the expansion of Horses Helping Humans so that many more lives can be touched. Glenys, you have continued to hold the finances and legalities of the HWYP charity in your hands and heart. You have been an absolute blessing.

To all my assistants, helpers and supporters over the years without whom I could not have managed it all – Kahli, Ruby, Debbie, Simmos, Chris, Belinda, Lu, Tracey, Giselle, Mel and Montana. And to my wonderful work experience students who have helped over the years, I'm so proud of you all!

To Brooke, for your beautiful photography. Thank you too, Elaine, for the support you have given us.

Thanks to Karen Phillips, Women in Business Awards Australia, for inspiring me to achieve goals beyond my dreams.

Also to Julie, from Bethyl Retreats, for teaching me 'I'm an eagle, not a chicken' and am capable of soaring.

To Ken Faulkner and Eliza Pridde, for taking me to a level of horsemanship that has allowed me to have a positive impact on so many young people.

Special thanks to Sharon Kolka, General Manager of Gwinganna Lifestyle Retreat, for sharing her beautiful horse Stevie with me.

And many thanks to Rita. Without your transcribing skills and your fast typing skills, I don't know how this book would have come together. Your patience and encouragement has been so appreciated.

To Dani, who typed in changes for my wonderful editor, you helped me make deadlines!

And Alex Craig, from Pan Macmillan Australia, who saw the big picture and asked me to tell it. Thank you so much.

And lastly, in special memory of 'Sam'.

2020 UPDATE

It is now 4 years since my book was published in Australia and New Zealand and to have it now available on worldwide bookstores is quite surreal.

We are all currently living through COVID 19 and all struggling in different ways to adapt our lives with restrictions and missing out on some of the simplest things like meeting friends for coffee or going to hear our favorite music played live or attending activities that helped us feel uplifted and connected.

Being cut off from loved ones, losing jobs, the list goes on but we must all take from this that feeling connected is the most important and valuable thing.

What stands out though this time is how the world has come together through technology.

To see people learning to Zoom, Skype and Face time so its possible to connect with someone anywhere in the world is heart warming. I feel it is what's holding so many people together right now.

The last 3 years have personally been so challenging, the heartbreaking loss of my beautiful Mum last year, the loss of one of my longest friends, my 28-year marriage ending. I felt like my world as I knew it had become unrecognizable.

My amazing Sunny at the age of 32 is now declining with neurological problems in his hind quarters. I have him in the only flat area we have as he can no longer walk down hills but he is being treated like a King! Everyday I just stand with him, our foreheads touching as I let him know how much I love him and if it wasn't for our journey Horses Helping Humans would not exist.

As he stands in the sun with his feeder full of the best feed he can look down into the little arena where he has helped thousands of young people and see his little herd still working their magic. The wisdom in his eyes and the love and gentleness he projects fills me with such emotion and thankfulness that this beautiful horse came into my life,

As he has helped so many over the years his constant presence has helped me through all my heartbreak over the past few years and I know the final goodbye is getting closer but what a legacy he will leave!

But through all the loss and grief light has shone in some areas like a rainbow on a cloudy day.

In spite of all the emotional challenges, over the past 3 years Horses Helping Humans has continued to grow with the most beautiful horsewomen and horseman becoming certified facilitators and delivering the program all over Australia and now in New Zealand.

The outcomes and testimonies they receive bring me to tears as they are replicating the magic of helping change peoples live.

The opportunities now to train people from anywhere in the world via on line training and videos is like a miracle to me.

I would always joke about Horses Helping Humans Worldwide but it is now becoming a reality and I am so proud!

Another incredible event is that this book ended up in the hands of Her Majesty the Queen and was read at Balmoral castle last year! I received a message of thanks from The Queen via the lady who sent it to her and lovely comments about how she was delighted to accept the book, which was a gift and thoroughly enjoyed hearing about the remarkable work I do with horses!

My Mum and Dad would have been so proud!

To see my youngest son jakes entertainment career as a professional magician flourished as Apollo Jackson, performing on major networks, large brand commercial campaigns as well as Australia's Got Talent, The Bachelorette and Bachelor in paradise has given me such joy during my challenging episodes.

His childhood dream continues to flourish. Releasing his own magic kit worldwide at the same time my book is being republished has brought such Joy.

My Mothers attitude of " Never Give Up " has influenced our whole family!

Which Horse OR Pony Are You has now also been published as a valuable recourse to help parents, teachers and counsellors understand which pony children relate to and how to introduce and normalise emotional health.

I love how my little herd is helping so many even in cartoon form far and wide!

I'd like to say a huge Thank You to all the readers who have contacted me since they have read my story. I am blessed to hear that sharing it has helped so many and that accepting ourselves allows others to feel accepted and heard, which is priceless.

Ingram Content Group UK Ltd.
Milton Keynes UK
UKHW011945140623
423431UK00001B/64